herein
is love

herein
is love

BY REUEL L. HOWE

A Study of the Biblical Doctrine of Love
in Its Bearing on Personality, Parenthood, Teaching,
and All Other Human Relationships.

JUDSON PRESS, VALLEY FORGE

International Standard Book No. 8170-0263-4

LIBRARY OF CONGRESS CATALOG CARD NO. 61-11105.

Printed in the U.S.A.

Sixteenth Printing, January, 1971

To my children

Marjorie and Lanny

FOREWORD

THIS BOOK WAS BORN out of a living encounter with the members of the Christian Education Conference to which I lectured at the American Baptist Assembly at Green Lake, Wis., in August of 1958. As I stepped to the speaker's rostrum to begin my first lecture to that group, and my first to so large a group of Baptist lay people, I wondered whether I as an Episcopalian and they as Baptists had images of each other that would help or hinder our communication. I shared with them my question and learned later they had been asking themselves the same question. I explained that I had prepared myself to speak to them in the hope that through me some of the truth of God would be heard by them, and I explained also that their lives were to be their preparation for hearing what I had to say; that is, that I hoped they would work as hard to hear me as I would work to make myself understood. They responded in good spirit, so that the Spirit of God spoke through and to all of us.

I describe this occasion because it produced the experience and context out of which the present book appeared. *Herein Is Love* is, I believe, an outward and visible sign of the fellowship of the Holy Spirit experienced on that occasion; and I offer it as a means of opening to others the possibility of participating in this fellowship of the Holy Spirit.

The theme of the book grows out of that experience: As the love of God required incarnation in Jesus of Nazareth in order that it might be received by us, so the Word of God's love in our day calls for persons in whom it may be embodied. The church, as the embodiment of divine love in human relationships, has tremendous responsibilities and opportunities in our modern culture. The old and familiar biblical symbols and stories do not always communicate their meanings to men today, and we must find a language that does. The language of the lived life of both man and God is the one that we shall use here in an attempt to open to us the meaning of the life of man and of God.

REUEL L. HOWE

January 10, 1961

CONTENTS

I

SOME FRIGHTENED FRIENDS

"There is no fear in love,
          but perfect love casts out fear."—*1 John 4:18*

"It seems to me that the church has lost its influence. Nobody pays much attention to it any more, except some of its own members; and they don't seem to be interested in anything except their own activities. The time was when the word of the minister carried weight. Some may not have agreed, but when the church spoke they paid attention. It's not true now, though."

Mr. Clarke eyed the others in the group as if he were testing their reactions to the statements he had just made. The church had always given him a sense of security, and now he was both worried that it seemed to have lost its power, and resentful that people no longer listened to its teaching.

He was one of a group of leaders of a local congregation who, at the request of their minister, were meeting to re-examine the purpose of the church. Not all of the group had arrived as yet, and the minister of the congregation, Mr. Gates, had been detained in his office by an emergency call upon his pastoral care.

Within the minute after Mr. Clarke finished, Mr. Wise spoke up. He was a thoughtful and compassionate member of the congregation who often raised the kind of questions that carried the discussion to deeper levels. When his questions were ignored, as they often were, he would smile good-naturedly and continue both as a contributor and as a question raiser. Turning to Mr. Clarke, he said: "I think I know how you feel. The statements of our ordained spiritual leaders are important, but do you think we should equate their words with—"

As usual, Mr. Wise's comment was interrupted, and this time by Mr. Churchill who, with evident irritation, protested against any concern over what others thought about the church. He said: "The church has got to be the church, and the world is different from it. I don't like this 'return to religion' business. Christianity and the church aren't supposed to be popular movements. If people want to join the church, that's fine; but if they don't, that's their lookout. Let's be the church and leave the world to itself."

"But why was Christ born *into the world*—" began Mr. Wise.

"I don't agree," exclaimed Mrs. Strait, responding to Mr. Churchill's comment and not hearing Mr. Wise. "I think we should be concerned about the world; concerned enough, at least, to set a good example, so that people will know what they're supposed to live up to and to do. After all, Jesus told us how we should live, and He did so in such simple words that even children can understand them. All we have to do—and it's written there for us to read—is to keep the commandments, imitate Jesus, and live a good life for ourselves and others."

"Yes, but if it's that simple, why don't church people live better—"

"Not at all! *Not at all!*" pronounced the stately Mr. Knowles with some disdain. "I don't agree with any of you. Our difficulties today result from the ignorance of our people, and the answer to the problem is education. We need to teach, and teach again. Church people must know their faith and know why they believe in it. When I was a child I was drilled thoroughly in the knowledge of the Bible, and I once won a prize for knowing more Bible verses than any other child. We need more adult education, and our children must be filled with the truth so they can recite it forwards and backwards. In my estimation, there is too much emphasis now on persons and not enough on the content of the faith."

"But didn't Jesus say, "For God so loved the world—"

"It seems to me," interrupted Professor Manby, "that all of you are in too much of a hurry. Some scientists estimate that man has been eight million years coming to his present state of life. In contrast, civilized man is only four thousand years old. This being true, we should be more patient. Given time, man will solve his problems."

"But has man's character developed in pace with his knowl—"

At that moment the Reverend Mr. Gates, with several other members of the committee, came into the room, and after greeting everyone he said: "Now let's get down to business. As you know, I've called this meeting in order that we may consider the purpose of our church in this community. I think we need a clearer understanding of why we are here. I wish we could be surer that we are serving God's purposes and not our own. I wish we all would assume as true that God's purposes for His church and for us are greater than anything we may think they are, and that we would hold our opinions and beliefs open to His correction and renewal."

"How can we be any clearer about the purpose of this church than to keep it open and its organizations going, so that people can come to it if they want to," exclaimed Mr. Churchill abruptly.

Mr. Wise now got to his feet, and with a twinkle in his eye began speaking: "You've all interrupted me several times, but now I'm going to speak my piece. I think Mr. Gates is right. We do need occasionally to rethink the reason for our existence as a church, lest it become a private club that caters to our own special needs. Our discussion so far tonight suggests that we want the church to be what we need it to be. We want God cut down to our own pattern and size. It may be that our church is too small for God, and that we'll turn out to be a religious, but godless, club."

"But how could that happen to us?" protested Mrs. Strait. "If we do what's right, God will love us and use us as His obedient servants."

"I wish Mr. Gates would set us straight on these matters. Were you going to say anything more, Pastor?" inquired Mr. Clarke.

"Yes, I'll have more to say," replied Mr. Gates slowly, "but this is not my problem only. That's why I called you together. We need to help each other think this question through. But to do that, we all shall need the spirit of Christ to help us. We need to look at the concepts and meanings that we bring out of our lives in the light of Christ's teachings and example. He brought the gift of God's love, but He brought also a judgment that was most disturbing to religious people. Instead of our judging what is good for Christ, I pray that He will judge us, and help us to be the instruments of His love."

"But you're our minister and teacher, so why don't you tell us what you think the job of the church is in this community? I'm sure we'd all support you in whatever you might suggest," urged Mr. Clarke.

"Mr. Clarke, I am not the church. I appreciate your confidence in me, but I am only one member of the church. The fact that I am ordained does not make me any more responsible for the church than you are, and I refuse to assume your responsibilities for you. Instead, I want to use my role as an ordained member of the church, and such training and experience as I have had, to help you find *your* role, so that together we can carry on the functions of the church in ways that will serve God and His people."

When Mr. Gates finished speaking there was silence. The reactions of his hearers were varied, showing anxiety, irritation, confusion, and blankness. And no wonder! The spontaneous discussion that had gone on before Mr. Gates' arrival had revealed how little their understandings of the church had prepared them to hear the question he was raising. The viewpoints they had brought to the meeting now closed their minds to the meanings he was trying to open to them.

What, then, were those concepts and meanings that made it so difficult for them to hear and understand their minister? Each of them represented a point of view that is widely prevalent in the church today and which keeps the church from being fully relevant and effective.

Clericalism

When Mr. Clarke thought about the church, he did so in terms of the clergy and their work in the church. We might call him a "clericalizer"; that is, one who thinks that only the minister does the work of the church. This idea is the basis of clericalism, the disease which saps the strength of the church because one part of the body, the ordained minister, is made to do the work of the rest of the body, the unordained members. In the discussion Mr. Gates took exception to this idea, and rightly so, for it results in a clergy that is overworked and frustrated. Indeed, they find it impossible to do all that needs to be done. And yet the idea has a hidden appeal for many of them, for it feeds their professional pride and arrogance. But the damage done by this disease does not cease there. It also makes for church people who are lazy, who feel that the church belongs to the clergy, and who are not themselves instruments through which God works in the world. God is kept from doing what He would do for them, because He cannot do through the clergy what He would do through the whole of His church.

Clericalism blocks the ministry of the church, because it tends to make lay members second-class citizens who feel incompetent on matters of religion. When the ordained member makes religious interpretation and action his professional monopoly, the lay member responds by exhibiting increasing ignorance and incompetence. Sometimes it seems as if lay people show less intelligence in the church than in their world. It is as though the practice of religion had a stupefying effect on them, whereas in other areas of living they are intelligent, informed, and perceptive. This clericalizing of the church's ministry produces in lay members the sense that religion is separate from life. They are heard to say to their ministers, "You stick to religion and leave the affairs of the world to us." Religion thus becomes a Sunday business, and Sunday business is kept separate from weekday business.

Still another and related ill effect of clericalism is that it keeps laymen from discovering the religious significance of their work.

Parents, for example, are not only parents entrusted with the physical, psychological, and social care of their children, but also are the teachers, pastors, and priests of their children. A teacher may serve God in his teaching, a doctor in his practice of medicine, a businessman in the conduct of his business, a milkman in the delivery of milk, and the garbageman in the collection of garbage. It is the business of the church to help these members find their ministry, but clericalism never allows them to make the discovery.

Clericalism, like any other concept, is more than a set of ideas. Mr. Clarke didn't just happen to hold that notion of the church. He held it because he needed it. His need grew out of his dependency, his timidity, and his fear of assuming responsibility. He needed to exalt the clergy. He wanted to be told what to believe and to do; and his "doctrine" of the ministry, namely, clericalism, justified him in his need. People who want to be told what to believe and to do inevitably will develop or drift toward a doctrine that is authenticated by their need.

Ministers also contribute to the prevalence of clericalism. All men have a very human and understandable need to be centrally important and indispensable, and ministers are tempted to exploit this need in the conduct of their work. It is only natural for them to think of the church as "my church," of the people as "my people," and of the ministry as "my ministry." These images cause them to function as if everything depended upon them, and as if they wanted everyone to depend upon them. Indeed, they may even measure the success of their ministry by the number of people who depend upon them for guidance and support, rather than by the number who are achieving mature self-sufficiency. As a part of this same picture, some ministers are unable to accept suggestions, much less criticism. The clericalized image they hold of themselves is that of an "answer man"; that is, one who has all the answers to human problems, and always right answers.

Thus, clericalism is a condition contributed to by both the ordained and the lay members of the church, and it tragically diminishes the power of the church. It is a symptom of Mr. Clarke's fear and of our own. It shows that we are afraid to trust God and to let His Spirit work through the whole of His people.

Churchism

Mr. Churchill's ideas, on the other hand, represented a different concept, one which may be called churchism, or pietistic other-worldliness, a concept which encourages the church's retreat from the world. It creates an artificial distinction between the religious and the secular, the religious being thought of as worship and all the other activities that go on in the church building, and the secular considered to be everything that goes on outside the building. In its local version churchism is parochialism, or total preoccupation with the church as an institution at the level of the local community.

The tragedy of such parochialism is that the creative thought and energies of people are consumed in the mere maintenance of the church as an institution, and in dead-end religious activity and worship. Mr. Churchill, and thousands of others who are like him, think of the church only as "gathered," as a congregation. They think that the church is most truly the church when its members are assembled in the church building and engaged in church work. They think of the church in terms of "going to church," of working for its organizations, of planning for its promotion, and of meeting the needs of the church as an entity separate from the rest of life. What is even worse, these people think that only when they are doing this church work are they serving God. Theologically, their concept means that Christ died for the church.

Instead, Christ died for the world! The purpose, then, of the church is not to meet its own needs but to serve God's purposes in the world. This forces upon us the position that not only should we think of the church in its *gathered* sense, but also in its *dispersed* sense. This means that church people should think of themselves as members of the church when they are out in the world, and that their work in the world is the means through which God may act through them in the accomplishment of His purposes. Therefore, in terms of the gathered church we can speak of "church work," but in terms of the dispersed church we must think of the "work of the church in the world," the work of the instrument of God's purposes there.

The relation between the gathered church and the dispersed church should be complementary. The church, as the people·of God, comes together in a conscious way from out of the world to be renewed, instructed, and equipped for the purpose of returning, as the body of Christ, to its task in the world. Then, out of its work in the world, the church gathers again to worship, to make its offerings, and to be strengthened anew for its work in the world. Elsewhere I have likened the church to an army that has been sent on a mission. In order to accomplish its purpose, it must have a base. In order to have a base, it must assign certain troops to the task of building and maintaining that base, so that the rest of the army may be free to accomplish its mission. We tend, however, to forget the "mission" and wastefully assign most of our people to building and maintaining bases, with the result that we do not accomplish our true purpose. More members need to be assigned to and trained for the mission, where the conflict between life and death goes on unceasingly.

Contrary to the opinion of Mr. Churchill, therefore, a complementary relation exists between the church and the world. The world is the sphere of God's action, and the church is the means of His action. The church must be found at work in the world, where it will encounter the tension between the saving purposes of God and the self-centered purposes of man.

As in the case of clericalism, so it is in the case of churchism. There is a human reason for the existence of the concept and for its prevalence in the church. The reason, in Mr. Churchill's case, was to be found in the conflict that he felt between his human interests and his church membership. He had certain real estate holdings and other investments from which he was making an excellent profit. Some of these, however, were exploitive and in contradiction to the faith which he professed. It was necessary, therefore, for him to keep the church and the world separate; and his doctrine of the church made it possible for him to rationalize the split between his faith and his life. We must not think that Mr. Churchill engaged in this contradiction deliberately. In part, his action was the unconscious means by which he held on to two conflicting values without suffering from the conflict between them. We must not think that Mr. Churchill is alone in this kind of separation of belief and practice, of splitting the church from the world. We all have our own individual forms of it.

It is because of our insecurity and fear that we develop these defensive attitudes of parochialism and churchism. We huddle like frightened children behind the doors of the church, whereas, as soldiers of Christ, we should be struggling courageously on the frontiers of life where the conflicts between love and hate, truth and prejudice, are being waged.

Moralism

The next member of the group who spoke up was Mrs. Strait, and she voiced for herself and for millions of other church people the moralistic understanding of the faith. Moralism is perhaps the most widespread of all the concepts that we are now discussing.

Moralism is usually identified as belief in good behavior as a source of life. A group of church people, many of them leaders of their respective parishes, were asked to describe the Christian. It would be no exaggeration to say that their descriptions of a Christian made it difficult to distinguish him from a Jew, because, according to their statements, a Christian is one who achieves his status as such by obeying the commandments of God. He must live a good life by keeping the law. The imitation of Jesus is the method, illuminated by a study of His teachings, especially the teachings in the Sermon on the Mount. And, as Mrs. Strait indicated, they agreed that a Christian should set a good example for other people.

When asked how they felt about this concept of the Christian life, many of them admitted that they were not too enthusiastic about it, because it was hard to achieve. They admitted that they failed often and miserably. One man put it rather well when he said that he felt that trying to be a Christian was like whistling in the dark. They all admitted that their concept was widespread among their fellow church members and that it had little appeal. When they were asked why such an unappealing concept of a Christian was so prevalent, they replied that it was due to people's feeling that they ought to be better than they are. Their discussion revealed further that they were unable to accept themselves as human beings, and that they felt they had to justify themselves by doing good works and by moral living.

That is the reason why Mrs. Strait holds to the moralistic concept of the Christian life. Separated from her husband and feared by her children, she feels acutely vulnerable and guilty. As a defense, she has built for herself a fortress made up of precepts, ideals, and rules, all based on a foundation of righteousness, and this has made her a formidable and rigid person. Like all self-righteous people, she tirelessly dispenses obvious truths, and keeps her own life and that of others narrowly proscribed.

Mrs. Strait is in no way an exception. The lives of moralistic people are not beautiful to behold. They are apt to be conventional, legalistic, and maintainers of the status quo. Because they have no sense of deliverance themselves, they are apt to be ungracious in relation to others. Because they live by the law, they do not show the fruit of the Spirit: namely, the love, joy, peace, and long-suffering which should mark the followers of Christ. They reveal how impossible it is for a human being to be a Christian by himself. He needs the spirit of Christ to live in him and to remake him. As we shall see later, there is available to us the spirit of Christ, who accomplishes in us the righteousness of Christ which is of the spirit and not of the law.

Moralism also is a sign of our fear and defensiveness. We reduce life to the dimensions of a moral code, because we are afraid to trust the Spirit and to risk the dangers of love and its communication. As one person said, "Let's be proper so we won't need to pray, for there is no knowing what God might ask us to do if we really listened to Him." In other words, moralism is a way of "playing it safe."

Intellectualism

A fourth concept sometimes held by church members about the faith was exhibited by Mr. Knowles. Its name is intellectualism. This intellectualism, sometimes called gnosticism, claims that knowledge is the source of life, and that the possession of knowledge delivers us from the power of evil. This is an ancient heresy that lives on in every generation. The desire to know and the achievement of skill in the use of knowledge are indeed commendable. But to know is not justifiable as an end in itself. Knowledge about God and man, about the Bible and the Christian faith, about the church and its history, is good and necessary for informed Christian living, but it can in no way substitute for our dependence upon Christ and the work of His spirit in us. We need to know about Christian faith, but it must not replace the need to love and to be loved. Knowledge *about* God must not become more important than our *knowing* God.

When religious and theological knowledge becomes an end in itself, the church is apt to become coldly intellectual and sophisticated. I am reminded of a group of laymen who became avid students of Christian theology, and who became so prideful in their achievement that they exhibited in their relations with one another, as well as with their other associates, a spirit of pride, arrogance, and competitiveness. They had acquired the knowledge of Christianity, but they had lost the spirit of the Christ.

The work of Christians is not so much to hold and transmit a knowledge of the faith as it is to be the personal representatives and instruments of Christ in the world. To be sure, Christ's representatives should know what they are talking about and intellectually be able to enter into dialogue with all men. But their knowing should incarnate them, both as persons and in their capacity to represent God and His Christ to men.

This brings us also ȷto a ̧controversy that exists in the field of Christian education. Many people feel that the purpose of the church school is to transmit the content of the Christian faith. Christian education, however, must be personal. It must take place in a personal encounter, and only secondarily is it transmissive. It is true, however, that Christian education is responsible for the continued recital of God's saving acts, and for the transmission of the subject matter of the historical faith and life of the Christian community. The content of our faith was born of God's action and man's response—a divine-human encounter. It is neither possible nor correct to reduce this to subject matter and substitute the transmission of subject matter for the encounter, with the assumption that it will accomplish the same purpose (it cannot, it never has, and it never will). Actually, the relations of transmission and encounter are complementary. Both are needed. The church, as the tradition-bearing community, contains both poles and should not subordinate one to the other. When the content of the tradition is lost, the meaning of the encounter is lost, and in the end even the encounter itself. Then tradition becomes idolatrous and sterile. Both are necessary to the community of faith, and both are meaningless, even dangerous, if separated. Christian teaching is concerned with both.

Mr. Knowles, however, is not happy about the required complementary relation between the content of the Christian faith and his life. As Mrs. Strait uses moralism for a defense, so Mr. Knowles uses his emphasis on the content of the Bible as a way of protecting himself from the deeper and more personal challenges of life. He is estranged from his family, and he is regarded as austere and unfriendly by his employees and many of his business associates. Personal relations frighten him, but by mastery of knowledge he gains superiority and power over others.

Intellectualism and gnosticism are not confined to the church. We see their influence in every walk of life. Many people *talk* much about the importance of love in human relationships, but they do not love. They use their knowledge *about* love as an evasion of their responsibility to express love. Man cannot be saved by what he knows, but only by the way he lives with his brother. "If any one says, 'I love God,' and hates his brother, he is a liar."[1] This is the stern but clear word of the Scriptures.

But we can be so frightened by the risks of expressing love that we may turn away from those who need our love and have a right to expect it from us. How much easier and safer it is to know *about* God and His love, and to confine this meaning to the sanctuary and the study group! Intellectualism, then, is another way in which we try to "play it safe."

Humanism

Professor Manby speaks for humanism, another point of view in the church. He, with others, says, "Give man time and he will work out his own salvation." Humanists, like Dr. Manby, often react against the religiosity of the church with the complaint that the search for truth is cluttered with obsolete myths and meaningless observances. On the other hand, the humanists, while splendid in their devotion to truth, have only their opinion of what is good and true to guide them. Because they acknowledge no life beyond this one, they become the servants of a closed system in which injustice frustrates the justice for which they plead and work. The plight of the humanists is pathetic. Since they accept no savior, they can draw only on their own human resources, and are put in the position of trying to lift themselves by their own power. They can only whistle in the dark. While man apart from God cannot save himself, God's love for the world works in the world, and He has a part for man to take. In the relation between God and man, there is need for both the greatness of God *and* the greatness of man.

[1] 1 John 4:20.

Dealing with Conflicts

And so these five frightened friends, familiar types to us all, reveal to us how easy it is to get lost in our preoccupations and to distort or diminish the truth we would serve.

Mr. Gates, the minister, has his anxieties, too. He represents the ordained ministry of the church, which is caught between the demands of the theory of Christianity and the demands of the world; between the demands of the pulpit and the demands of the pew; between the church as an institution and the church as a saving power in the world; between the surges of the spirit and the sucking drag of tradition. And he himself is also trapped by the demands of his image of himself as a minister and the demands of his people's image of him; by the idealism of his training for the Christian ministry and the realism of the demands on his ministry in the church and in the world.

He cannot resolve these conflicts by himself, nor should he try. These are not his conflicts. They are the conflicts of the church's ministry, and he and the people need to deal with them together. Neither he nor they will be able to resolve the conflicts, because they are the inevitable tensions between the spirit and the law, and between life and form. But Mr. Gates and all other ministers, together with the rest of the people of God, by reason of the Christian faith, must live through these conflicts and deal with them creatively.

Both Mr. Gates and his people need to accept conflicts as an inevitable part of life, especially of a life that is lived in response to a call or a loyalty. No growth or learning takes place at any depth without such conflict: conflict between the known and the unknown, between our need for security and our need for maturity. This is the nature of life. As for the gospel, let us not forget that its universally accepted symbol is the cross, a symbol of the conflict between love and hate, between life and death. As Christians, our only realistic expectation is that because of our Christian belief and practice, our conflicts will increase and intensify rather than diminish. The only peace we may hope to have is an irrational peace, an "in-spite-of" peace, the peace of the depths beneath the storm-tossed surface; in other words, "the peace of God, which passes all understanding." [1] To suggest how this may be achieved in some areas of life is the purpose of this book.

Finally, Mr. Wise, the member of the group whose remarks were always being interrupted by the others, represents a Christian point of view which, in the church generally, is listened to no more than it was here. What he was trying to say will be explored more fully as an answer to some of the questions raised in this chapter.

[1] Phil. 4:7.

II

GOD IN THE WORLD

"For God so loved the world
that he gave his only Son. . . ."—*John 3:16*

THE CONCEPTS AND attitudes of Mr. Clarke, Mr. Churchill, Mrs. Strait, Mr. Knowles, and Professor Manby lead them and the rest of the church away from God and the world. Their clericalism, pietism, moralism, intellectualism, and humanism represent ways in which frightened and disturbed people seek to make themselves secure. Unfortunately, however, their security then is purchased at the price of their freedom. Their lives become locked up in the small closet of their limited concepts. Their literal and rigid understanding of the Christian church and its faith makes them so loveless that their lives have an alienating effect on others, and they themselves fail to find God.

Concepts About God May Be Dangerous

They do not, nor shall we, find God in our concepts about Him or about His church. He is not to be found in assertions about Him or in abstract belief about His omnipotence or other attributes. God is not an idea, but Being itself, and our ideas are only our concept or image of Him. When we confuse God with our ideas about Him, we are misled into thinking that we know what He wants, and we tend to represent and act for Him uncritically. This confusion between God and our ideas about Him explains why the religion of so many people lacks humility and reverence. It is one of the reasons why true Christian fellowship is as rare as it is.

Not only may these ideas and concepts lead us away from

26

God, but also they may lead us out of the world and away from that encounter with the world which began with the Incarnation. Separation of the church from the world, its assumption that its task is to defend itself from the attacks of the so-called secular, its defensiveness of God in response to the unfaith of the world, all are symptoms of church people's lack of faith in God and of their failure to understand how and where He works. In other words, the otherworldliness of the church hardly harmonizes with the worldliness of God, Who chose to create the world, to speak and act in and through it, and Who finally entered it and made the life of man in history His right hand. Our belief in the Incarnation and our understanding of the love of God for the world should send us, as children of God, into the world, into the so-called secular order, eager to participate in its meanings, and to bring them into relation with the meanings of God.

As we work at this, we shall begin to experience true Christian fellowship, the fellowship of the Holy Spirit, which I understand to be the fellowship of people who have the courage to live together as persons rather than to relate themselves to each other through their ideas and preconceptions. Christian fellowship is living with and for one another responsibly, that is, in love. "If any one says, 'I love God,' and hates his brother, he is a liar." [1] And, "He who abides in love abides in God, and God abides in him." [2] If we would find God, therefore, and learn the meaning of life and love, we must live in the world by giving ourselves to one another responsibly. It is for this that the church exists. The church does not exist to save, build up, and adorn itself. Nor does it exist to protect or defend God. The mission of the church is to participate in the reconciling dialogue between God and man. Here is the source of the true life of the world. Here, too, is the source of the life of the church and its worship. Without this, everything, including worship, is false and idolatrous.

[1] 1 John 4:20.
[2] 1 John 4:16.

These are some of the things which Mr. Wise was trying to say
to the group. He represents those in the church who see beneath
the surface of things and behind the distortions of conventional
and defensive Christianity. But the question that finally emerges
is: How do we free ourselves from the distortions of our faith?
What should we do?

We Find God at Work in the World

The answer is simple. We should look for God in the world.
We shall find Him in the meeting between men. "Where two
or three are gathered in my name, there am I in the midst of
them." [1] And, "gathered in my name" means gathered in the
spirit and after the character of Jesus. It does not mean gathered only under special and separate religious auspices. To be
sure, the gatherings of God's people for worship and instruction are indispensable to the life of the church, but unless we
translate our worship and instruction into action, our religious
observances will be idolatrous and sinful, and will separate men
from each other and from God. So we look for God where He
works; that is, in the world and between man and man.

The place where we encounter God first, in the course of our
individual lives, is in the family. The family provides the individual with his first experience of living in relation to other
persons, and this is his first experience of Christian fellowship.
Immediately we are confronted with the nature of God's creation
and, therefore, with the revelation of Himself and of how He
works. We are confronted with the relational nature of all life;
for nothing exists in isolation. Everything and every person finds
full meaning only in relation to other things and persons.

We are used to thinking of persons as living in relation to persons; we are less accustomed to thinking of things existing in
relation to other things. But does not the tree exist in relation to
the earth, atmosphere, and water? And does not the hammer exist
as hammer in relation to the hand that uses it and the object it

---

[1] Matt. 18:20.

pounds? The only difference is that persons are active participants in relationship and things are passive. But things may be made active symbols or instruments in the meeting between man and man, as, for instance, in the case of the bread and wine of the Lord's Supper.

God created man to live in relation with the world of things, with himself, and with his fellow men, and to live in these relationships in such a way that he will discover and grow in his relationship with God. The terms "man" and "relationship" are synonymous. An old Roman proverb puts it, "One man is no man at all." Alone we would cease to exist. We all have had the experience of being shut out from some important relationship and we know what a desperate feeling it produces. We lose whatever sense of well-being we may have had, and we begin to feel unwanted, depressed, and less alive. When we are warmly gathered again into an important group, we begin to come alive. Our blood runs faster, and we know the joy of life again. It is almost as though we had been resurrected. The sense of being a part, the experience of fellowship, makes the difference between life and death. I once visited in a home where a teen-age girl was having one of her frequent "tragic" love experiences. The boy she was currently dating had not called her up for three days. She was full of gloom, moped around the house, and lost her usual interest in everything. One evening the phone rang and the call was for her. First we heard her laugh, and then she burst into the room full of gaiety and enthusiasm. You would not have known her for the same girl. Alone and rejected, as she thought, she was dead. Restored to relationship, she came alive again. We may smile patronizingly at the emotional excesses of this teen-age girl, but on the other hand we understand deeply the fundamental meaning of her experience.

The patterns of relationship begin with our birth. We would not survive if the whole community, centering in the basic function of the mother, did not assume responsibility for us. Our dependence upon her for food and care is the occasion for the beginning of relationship. And both the infant and the mother have their part to play. She moves as a person toward her child with the gifts of her milk and of her love. The infant, on his side, in random and non-specific ways, calls out to her. He cries and makes his simple movements. She responds to his cries with her care. He responds to her care by sleeping and waking, by crying and cooing. And thus begins the dialogical nature of relationship.

Relationship Is Dialogue

Relationship is dialogue. Dialogue occurs when one person addresses another person and the other person responds. It is a two-way process in which two or more people discuss meanings that concern them. To whatever degree one part of the dialogue is lost, to that degree the relationship ceases to exist. A marriage, for instance, ceases to exist, except in form, only when either one of the partners ceases to communicate with the other, and the quality of address and response is lost. Likewise, true religion disappears when it represents only what God says and eliminates the meaning of man's response. Religious dogma is sometimes used to shackle human creativity, and the form of belief is allowed to stifle the vitality of faith. Similarly, religion disappears when the address to God and the response of God are eliminated. The Pharisee in Jesus' parable had lost the dialogical quality of his prayer because he "stood and prayed thus with himself. . . ." [1] He was not speaking to God and he expected no response, with the result that his religion lost its dialogical quality since he was separated from God by his self-righteousness. This dialogical quality is indispensable to creative living. It is out of the dialogical encounter that the individual emerges.

Only by the process of dialogical teaching can children really learn. The relationship between parent and child is not one-sided. The child may protest against the authority of the parent. This is the child's part of the dialogue. The parent may recognize his child's need to find himself as an autonomous person by making

[1] Luke 18:11.

allowance for his protest and exercise of freedom. The next stage in the dialogue between them is the reassurance which the child experiences and reflects in his behavior in response to his parent's affirmation of him as a person. He may show this by a more realistic acceptance of the parent's authority. This in turn may reassure the parent, so that he feels more relaxed in the exercise of his authority. Gradually the parent and the child begin to experience a more mature relationship with each other.

We Are Responsible for Each Other

Because of the dialogical nature of relationship, we have responsibility for one another. Each of us has a responsibility to call forth the other as a person, and each needs to be called forth since none of us will develop automatically. We call forth one another in the same way that the conductor of an orchestra calls forth the powers of his musicians and the potentialities of their instruments. And they respond by calling forth the interpretive genius of their conductor. Each draws out the powers of the other.

The potentialities for development are inherent in us, but we need the warmth and stimulation of other persons. This is certainly true in the case of the newly born. The role of parents and teachers is to call forth and welcome the personal responses and initiatives of their children. This is also true of those who, because of the pressures of life, start to unfold as persons but then withdraw in order to protect themselves from further hurt. Here again, parents and teachers, pastors and counselors, and indeed all men, from time to time, are obliged to call forth some soul who is either in hiding or in retreat.

This role is easy to see in our relation with children, because children's responses are sometimes so uncomplicated that the process we are talking about is clearly revealed. Susie, feeling that an injustice had been done her, retreated to her room and withdrew into herself. After seeing that she would need help in order to come to herself again, her mother finally asked her if she would like to help her bake a cake. Soon Susie and her mother were chatting happily together in the kitchen doing something that Susie loved to do whenever her mother had time to help her. During the course of their conversation, the mother had an opportunity to help Susie understand the situation that had upset her. As a result, Susie emerged out of the situation more mature and resourceful.

I once knew a bus driver who discovered that he, too, could call forth people by the way in which he greeted them and did business with them. On his morning runs he observed that many people were grumpy and sullen, and treated him and their fellow passengers discourteously. At first his inclination was to respond in the same way. Then he discovered that by taking the initiative and greeting his passengers with a smile and cordial word, and by making change cheerfully and being patient with their grumpiness, the spirit of his passengers underwent a transformation. Over the years a number of people told him how grateful they were for his good cheer. They said that his influence had often been decisive in their lives. It had affected their relations with other people. Thus, his attitude toward people and his method of relating himself to them as a driver of a bus became his ministry; and since he was a member of the church, the church's ministry reached out and worked through that bus driver into the lives of many who may never have come anywhere near the church. Through such relationships, God is present and active in the world.

The relationship between man and man, therefore, not only is important to men, but also is a part of God's plan for the reconciliation of the world unto Himself. It is given to us for our own sakes and also for the accomplishment of God's purposes. Unfortunately, however, our relating to one another often is hurtful because of our anxiety and insecurity. We may attack others in order to make ourselves feel secure. Instead of calling them forth, we cause them to withdraw. Even when we undertake to love others, we may do it in ways that hurt them, because we love them for selfish reasons. Human relationships, in themselves, are ambiguous, and we need deliverance from the ambiguity of them, for these relationships can either destroy people or call them forth.

Human Love Is Ambiguous

Furthermore, because human love can be ambiguous, we do not know whether it is safe to give and accept love. It is a risk both to love and to accept love, and all of us, to some degree, are afraid to take the risk. Some people, to be sure, have more courage for it than others. They love more courageously, and are more courageous in their acceptance of others' love. These people seem to have a power of being that others lack.

The giving and receiving of love implies responsibility for one another, and we may withhold our love and reject the love of others as a way of evading the responsibility of love. We are willing to love up to the point where it begins to be inconvenient to love any more. We like the image of ourselves as loved and loving people, but we would like the benefit without the responsibilities of the role. When the response to our love presents us with demands, we may begin to hold people off. We may say: "Yes, to be sure, I love you, but keep your distance. I am willing to give of myself, but not too much. I need to keep something of me for myself." By this attitude we are admitting that when we love another we have to give ourselves to him, entrust ourselves to him. Commitment to another person is a courageous act, and it is no wonder that we sometimes recoil from it.

What has been said about giving love is equally true of accepting love, for the acceptance of love also calls for trust and commitment. If I really respond to your love, I will open myself to the possibility of being hurt because your love cannot be completely trusted. Furthermore, if you should really love me, I am not worthy of your love and I do not welcome the judgment of me that is implicit in your love. I shall, therefore, make a cautious response to you and give myself to you guardedly. Then the person who is giving love is made lonely because his gift is not accepted. He, too, begins to withdraw and to dole out his love, which in turn increases the anxiety of the one to whom it is being given. This is an aspect of human fellowship which we need to recognize before we talk much about Christian fellowship. Human fellowship is both heroic and tragic; it is both renewing and destructive; it is both healing and hurtful, but it is indispensable to life. This is our human predicament.

Something is needed to cut into the ambiguity of human love. And this is what Christ does. He draws the confused currents of human love into the unifying stream of divine love, thus making possible a new relationship. As the apostle Paul makes clear, we become new creatures in Christ, and as such, a part of a new creation.[1]

Having considered some of the characteristics of human love and fellowship, let us now look at Christian love and fellowship. One word of caution is needed before we begin. The fellowship of Christian men and women will still have its human look, but something new has been added that makes a difference. What is it? How shall we describe the new relationship?

What Is Christian Fellowship?

Christian fellowship is the relation of men and women who, by the power of the Holy Spirit, participate in the life and work of Christ. Christian living is participation in the continued living of Christ through the activity of His Spirit. This concept stands in sharp contrast to the ones held by the church members described in the first chapter. The source of the Christian's life is not knowledge about God or even our historical remembrance of His incarnate life, although they contribute to it. Neither is it to be found in a determined imitation of Christ's life, although that effort also will help. Nor is it in the good will of man which, along with his power of love, is likewise found to be ambiguous. No, the true source of the Christian life and of the

[1] See 2 Cor. 5:17.

Christian relationship is the incarnation of His Spirit in the lives of men. The presence and working of His Spirit transforms our own spirit and provides a new dynamic for our living. This does not mean that we cease to be human; the old conflicts are still there and the old battles must continue to be fought, but a new power of being and of love is given to us by the indwelling Spirit.

Just now we referred to the incarnation of His Spirit in us. The concept of incarnation is an ancient one in Christianity, and represents the embodiment of God in the human form of the historic Jesus, Who participated in the life of man as man in order that man, through Him, might participate in the Being of God. What happened is known to us all. The incarnation produced the life of Jesus, His death, resurrection, and the coming of His Spirit. These are not once-for-all historic events as was the life of Julius Caesar or of George Washington. Through Him a new power of love was released into life that continues unto this day. B.C. and A.D. are not merely a way of dividing time, but are our way of acknowledging that in the life of Jesus of Nazareth something radically different entered into life, a new dynamic that changed the nature of creation. We participate in the historic incarnation of Jesus of Nazareth which took place 1900 years ago by the daily incarnations of His Spirit in our individual lives and in the life of the people of God. And since His incarnation meant God's entry into the world, so likewise the indwelling of His Spirit in us also should mean God's entry into our world and into its conflicts and issues.

We are Christians by doing what He did in the world, which was to have a care and a responsibility for others. His Spirit seeks to incarnate Himself in the day-to-day decisions of every responsible person in every sphere of his living. Thus the mother not only serves God by her decisions and actions in the home, but through these same decisions and actions she may believe that God is present and accomplishing His purposes for her and for the members of her family. So, likewise, a businessman's sphere of Christian action is carried out in the decisions and work of his business, but also he may believe that in and through these same decisions and work God seeks to accomplish His purpose. So the principle of incarnation means that God is both served and met at the points of decision and responsibility of our daily lives. And this is what it means to participate in His life by the power of His Spirit, to bear the true mark of the Christian.

In the context of these thoughts, we may now look at the three parts of the earthly life of Jesus Christ, and, as we examine them, the idea of participating in His life may become clearer.

Participation in the Life of Christ

First of all, there is His earthly life, the life of the man Jesus, Whom we call Lord and Savior, the Christ. This life gives us the picture of what God meant man to be. Here is the perfect portrait of God's creation—man. It is a stirring picture and we love to look at it, contemplate it, read about it. It is a dull mind and heart that does not quicken in response to His amazing compassion and strength; and as we study his instructions to us, it becomes clear that He expects us to be to our generation what He was to His.

When we realize what His teaching and commandment require of us, our sense of the beauty and simplicity of His life is overshadowed by the terror aroused in us by His expectation of us. We know that the ugliness of our lives can never reproduce the beauty of His. From a human point of view, the imitation of Christ is a complete impossibility, and one wonders how so many Christians can go on, generation after generation, thinking that this is their task and that they can accomplish it. Yet it is clear that He expects us to be members of His body and to do His work in our time. Is it possible that He asked us to do something that is beyond our powers of accomplishment? If this is so, then far from being Savior, He is one of the most cruel of men. There must be some other answer.

The answer, of course, is that Christ did not leave us alone to carry out His commandments, summed up in the great commandment: "You shall love the Lord your God with all your heart, and with all your soul, and with all your strength, and with all your mind; and your neighbor as yourself." [1] He understood only too well the ambiguity of our lives. How understanding He was of vacillating Peter, and yet He called him the Rock. Had Peter possessed any self-understanding, he must have wondered why his Lord gave him that name. But after the resurrection and the coming of the Holy Spirit, Peter became the Rock, because then he incarnated the Spirit of his Lord. As with Peter, so with us. The presence of the Spirit makes possible an imitation of Christ. Now we can read the Gospels without dread, and not as patterns for us to imitate literally and slavishly. The New Testament provides the understandings that help us to test whether or not we are responding to His Spirit and letting Him accomplish His work in and through us. Thus, like Peter, we may become rocks, incarnating the Spirit of our Lord.

Nor do we need to be embarrassed by our humanity. We begin to sense that we cannot be Christian without first being human, which means that we shall be both loving and hostile, both righteous and sinful, both courageous and cowardly, both dependable and vacillating. We are in the world and of the world as other men are, and we share the lot of human existence. But in addition, we have been given the spirit of power and love and self-control, not that we may be condescending toward the world, or try to regulate it as if it were a recalcitrant child, but that we may be embodiments of the Spirit of God in human affairs through whom He may accomplish His purposes in the world. In the process, because His Spirit is in us, men will know that they have seen Jesus.

Thus we may come to understand the life of the people of God, and to find therein a basis for a true evangelism; and thus we may participate in the life and teaching of Christ, which are at once our ideal and pattern of living, and at the same time our judgment.

[1] Luke 10:27.

Participation in the Crucifixion

Since the life of the Christian is participation in his own time in the life of Christ, he must participate also in the crucifixion and death of his Lord, which were a part of His life. Christ's crucifixion and death were a natural consequence of His teaching and of the way in which He lived. The acceptance of the unacceptable, the loving of the unlovable, inevitably produces the necessity of the Cross, which itself must be chosen and accepted if the life of love is to be triumphant.

We would like to evade this part of Christian living, if that were possible. The Cross and all that it represents is the part of the Christian gospel that we would prefer to skip. The lives of church people reveal only too clearly how much they wish it were possible to move directly from the contemplation of the ideal to its actualization, and to bypass the experience of crucifixion and its meaning for us. Lovers, for example, would like to move from the contemplation of the romantic ideal of their love to its realization in their lives. But the full meaning of their love cannot become available to them except as they pass through the challenges and crises of their relationship and die to themselves for the sake of the other. Nor can anyone master a skill or a field of study except as he moves from the vision of what he *might* do, to its realization through the path of self-discipline, which is a kind of dying to himself and to other values which he might choose and cultivate.

Jesus Christ affirmed by His teaching and life this principle of disciplined self-giving. If we would be partakers of His resurrection, we must be willing to be buried with Him in His death. We are expected to show forth His death till He comes, and we do this by dying daily. In one sense, the life of the Christian is a life of dying. Being buried with Christ in His death is symbolized in the act of baptism, especially when it is administered by immersion and accompanied with such a Scripture verse as, "We were buried therefore with him by baptism into death, so that as Christ was raised from the dead by the glory of the Father, we too might walk in newness of life." [1] In other words we have to expect the pain of our relationships and accept the responsibility of them for the sake of the glory in them that may be revealed later. We are to accept the unacceptable in ourselves and in others, because on the cross Christ accepted the unacceptable in all men. This is what produced the Cross. And so He died, bearing the sin of man while He perfectly fulfilled His own teaching; that is, He was perfectly obedient to the full meaning of love. We too have to die daily to our desire for peace at any price, to our desire to work out convenient and comfortable compromises, and to our desire to be God and to have things run our own way. Thus, we come to realize the meaning of His words, "Whoever loses his life for my sake and the gospel's will save it." [2]

The Christian fellowship, therefore, is the fellowship of men and women who accept dying as a part of living, and who are not surprised by the presence in human relations of selfishness, betrayals, misrepresentations, hostility, and all other violations of the ideal. When we meet these things, we should not run away, or pretend that such conditions do not exist. Instead, we should face these hostile and negative human responses with courage. Because we are participating in the life of our Lord, we may move through these experiences, knowing that nothing can really separate us from the love of God which seeks to make itself known in and through our relations with one another. We may trust that if we accept the pain that we have in our relations with one another and are obedient to the spirit of the love that seeks to reunite man with man, we may emerge on the farther side of the painful experience with relationships that are richer, deeper, and stronger than they were before.

An excellent illustration of this principle is to be found in Tennessee Williams' play, *Cat on a Hot Tin Roof,* the point of which many people miss because of what they regard to be the

[1] Rom. 6:4; See also Col. 2:12.
[2] Mark 8:35.

vulgarity, profanity, and licentiousness of its characters. In the play, Brock, the son, evaded his problems with himself, his father, his wife, and his work through an excessive use of alcohol. His father, Big Daddy, in his rough, profane way was greatly concerned about his son. Finally, in a tremendous scene between Big Daddy and Brock, the father pursued his son through every kind of evasion and rationalization in a determined effort to break through to his heart. Nothing that Brock could say to his father was sufficient to cause Big Daddy to turn away. He could easily have abandoned his sick boy and evaded the pain of what he was trying to do. Instead, he hammered at the door of Brock's life with a love that was willing to accept every rejection that his son could offer. And he did not give up. Finally, he broke through, reached his boy, and brought him back to his life with his family and his work. Because he was willing to die to himself and every comfortable impulse, Big Daddy was freed to be the instrument of a saving love. Here was a dramatic portrayal of the truth which our Lord not only taught but exemplified, and which He would like to see reproduced in the lives of all of us.

Incidentally, it is ironical that so many Christian people missed the real message of this play because they were so easily offended by that which is not pretty in human life. It is a shame that we would rather be pretty than redemptive. We seem to place respectability above salvation. Christians ought to be able to see through and behind the dirty and sinful ways in which people live, and recognize them as symptoms of a spiritual condition that calls for that which God is trying to give them through us. It is tragic that some would-be Christians, like Mrs. Strait, become so moralistic that they condemn rather than help people. Christ could see behind the suffering of men, behind their sins, and He was not distracted by what they did. He was concerned for men first and for their behavior last. He knew that if He could reach the man, the behavior would take care of itself. We are supposed to be like Him, men and women who, because His Spirit indwells us and because we participate in His living and dying, are able to see the hearts of other men and women and to unite them with the power of God's love and forgiveness.

Participation in the Resurrection

This kind of living would bring us to our third participation in the life of Christ, namely, in His resurrection. Because He was faithful to His love and willing to die in obedience to its demand, He was raised up in triumph, and with Him all things were made new. These were the events of His life. But His life affirms the principle of God's life as it is lived in human existence. Since His Spirit incarnates itself in us, then we may expect that our lives will be triumphant also and be the source of renewal for others. Another criticism that we can make of Christians is that they do not have this sense of expectancy, this sense of deliverance, this sense of triumph, and this appearance of having been renewed. All too often we are grim and sad, discouraged and cynical, and our lives contradict the faith we profess.

However, because we participate in His resurrection, we are given the wonderful power of facing any problem with courage, even though it may seem, from a human point of view, that no solution is possible. We live in the faith that if we consent to be buried with Christ in His death, we shall be made partakers of His resurrection. And this, not in the hereafter, but now, in this present life.

A father told me of an incident with his son that illustrates the principle we are now considering. He and his son had become involved in a quarrel and both had lost their tempers. The father confessed that he had said some harsh and cruel things to his boy. Finally, however, he came to himself, realized what he was doing, and, dying to his pride, he acknowledged his fault and asked his son's forgiveness. When the exchange was over, the boy was still rather subdued, but later when he came through the room where his father was seated, he called out cheerily, "Hi, Pop." The cheerful greeting of the son was a sign of the triumphant relationship between father and son, and, in the human relationship, the father was participating in the resurrection of Jesus Christ.

In other words, our participation in the life, death, and resurrection of Christ will give us courage, faith, and hope. This way of life will not save us from the pain of human living, nor will it save us from going through dark times of indecision and lack of faith. We shall, however, be able to live our lives out of the power of the triumphant life that God lived in human life.

Our worship is yet another way in which we participate in the life, death, and resurrection of our Lord. In worship we bring our lives to the judgment of Christ's teaching and life, and these reveal how unequal we are to live His life, and how greatly we need His Spirit to transform our lives. By our confession of our sins we participate in His death for us and for our sins, and the assurance of His forgiveness enables us to participate in His resurrection so that we may rise to our feet, make a confident offering of ourselves, and sing our praises of thanksgiving.

The Christian, we conclude, is one in whom the Spirit of Christ is incarnate. By the power of the Spirit he participates in the life of Christ, so that the presence of Christ and His Spirit has contemporary power and meaning in the arena of human relations. The love of God is for the world, and this world-love of God should be reflected in the devotion of His people to His work in the world.

III

HEREIN IS LOVE

"Beloved, let us love one another; for love is of God, and
he who loves is born of God and knows God."—*1 John 4:7*

THUS FAR, WE HAVE IDENTIFIED the Christian life as participation in the life of Christ, and the Christian fellowship as the relationship of men who have been reunited to one another by the presence in them of the Spirit of Christ. We need to make this concept even more specific and, therefore, now ask the question: "How does one participate in the life of Christ; how does one find the Spirit; what must one do?" The gospel's answer is: "You shall love."[1] It has surpassing attraction, but is also considerably disappointing. Love is appealing, but its practice is appallingly difficult. While the Christian relationship seems to promise a difference, it is hard to identify. What makes the difference? or, What is the Good News?

The Gift of God in Christ

Christians believe that the gift of God in Christ confers something that man needs but has lost. What is it that we do not have that we are supposed to receive as a result of our new relationship with Christ? Let us recall that in our earlier discussion we took note of the ambivalent character of love. We want to be loved and we are afraid to accept love; we want to love and are afraid to give love for fear it will not be accepted. We are not free to love, therefore; that which by nature we cannot have is the freedom to love. We believe that God is love. Creation is the work of His love, and love is the work of His

[1] Luke 10:27.

43

creation. But the ambivalences of human nature keep us from being free in the work of love. The coming of Christ, in the midst of history, changed the balance of power between love and hate, life and death, and set us free to love. Love became the energizing, reconciling force in human existence. B.C. and A.D. marked the transition, not only of time, but also of the old creation in which our power of love was imprisoned in our fear to love, and of the new creation in which our power of love was set free by the love of God in Christ. Now the triumphant power of God's love is at work in the world and is available to all who seek to do the work of love anywhere and for anyone. Accordingly, the work of love was and is the breaking down of walls of separation, and the reuniting of man and God, man and man, and man with himself, in all which work we participate.

What Is Love?

Do we know what we mean when we think of love in this way? A clear understanding of love is needed, because it is so gravely misunderstood in our time. All too commonly, love is regarded as a sentiment, a feeling, a "liking" for someone. While sentiment and emotion are certainly a part of love, it is tragic to make them synonymous with love. Certainly we mean more than that when we say, "God is love," or when we wrestle with the concept of man showing his love of God through his love for his neighbor. In these concepts we are thinking of love as the moving, creating, healing power of life; of love that is "the moving power of everything toward everything else that is."[1] Love reunites life with life, person with person, and as such is not easily discouraged. The most dramatic symbol of love's courage and triumph is, as we have seen, the cross and the resurrection; it stands for the love wherewith God has loved us. "In this is love, not that we loved God but that he loved us...."[2] Having given

---

[1] From *Love, Power and Justice,* by Paul Tillich, Oxford University Press, Copyright, 1954. Used by permission.

[2] 1 John 4:10. The title of this book was suggested by the familiar opening words of this verse in the King James Version, "Herein is love. . . ."

us His love, we have it for our response to Him, so that we love Him by loving one another with His love which we received through His people. Thus, the nurturing of our response to God's love is the work of the church. Our responsibility is to love Him. We are to love God by loving one another, and in loving one another we introduce one another to God. This is the work of the church and the vocation of the people of God. We are called to love one another reunitingly with the love wherewith God loved us.

In order for us to participate in the love of God which is at work in the world, we need to understand ourselves and our own creaturely problems in relation to love. Too much Christian thought about love and its work is abstract rather than a reckoning with the complications of human existence. In order to avoid this danger, let us turn to a consideration of what is involved in recovering our freedom to love.

Recovering Our Freedom to Love

Because we are created in the image of God, our deepest need is to be loved. This need is fundamental and has both human and divine roots. The baby comes into being as a result of being loved. We take him in our arms, care for him, call him by name, and reveal to him the love that we have for him. Thus he experiences love. These experiences of love stimulate, in turn, his love, which is the completion of his need of love. His response to being loved is to love, and this response is not long in coming. We see it in his smiles, in his cooing, when he pats his mother's cheek, when he puts his little arms around her neck, and later when he begins to toddle and bring his gifts to her. In many ways the individual begins to show that he has been loved by revealing his growing power to love.

Our day, however, seems to be one in which people are more conscious of their need to be loved than of their need to love, with the result that everyone is running around looking for love. But we do not find love by looking for it; we find it by giving it.

And when we find love by loving, we find God. Our Lord gave us His love generously, not in order that we might be loved, but that we might be freed to love one another. "You received without pay, give without pay." [1] He calls us from our childish preoccupations with security to the appropriate adult occupations of the mature Christian. He calls us away from our suckling tendencies to our responsibility to feed others, from receiving to giving. If someone came to me and asked, "How can I find God?" I would answer, "Go find someone to love and you'll find Him."

Unless the searcher was love-deprived and in need of reassurance, I would not begin by figuratively putting my arm around him and cherishing him. There are situations where this is necessary. People can be so broken and so hurt that they cannot love, and they need to be cherished and reassured until they can. One of the responsibilities of the church is to be on the alert for those people who in later life need the love and reassurance they should have had when they were younger. Unfortunately, however, many of us are embarrassed when we are confronted by emotionally needy persons. We may resent their need and the demand which it makes on us, with the result that they may never know the love of man and God, and may never be brought to the point where they may participate in the life and work of Christ which is, as we have seen, to love.

Of course, it is not easy to love, especially when we feel unequal to it, are tempted to regress, and want to be loved and cuddled ourselves. Yet even then the answer to our need is to love. Many of us have had experiences that have borne out this truth. Once when my son and I had had a quarrel in which I had lost my temper, and was feeling discouraged as a father and not at all competent where human relations were concerned, the phone rang and a young couple asked if they might come and talk with me about the difficulty they were having with their young son. Because of my feelings of wretched inadequacy, my

[1] Matt. 10:8.

inclination was to say "No," but they were so obviously in need of help and so importunate that I arranged for them to come to see me immediately. I had no confidence in being able to help them, but I did try to listen to them. As I listened, I participated in their thinking about their own situation. When the session was over, they thanked me enthusiastically for my help. After they were gone, I realized that however much I had helped them, I myself had been helped. By accepting my responsibilities as a counselor and by listening to them, I was loving them; and because I loved them, I had the experience of being loved. The relationship in which our love is needed may offer little apparent encouragement, but once we give ourselves, the resources for the work of love become available.

It is, therefore, as important for us to love as it is for us to be loved, and our need to love is as great as the need to be loved. If we are not able to love, life is as deficient as it would have been if we had not been loved. We must not assume that because we have been loved we shall automatically become a person who loves. Human beings do not develop that automatically. Certainly the experience of being loved prepares us to love, but we can misuse the gifts of love. We may decide to appropriate them for ourselves. We may not want to assume responsibility for others. But having received love and choosing not to love, we may lose such love as we have. We then become self-centered and selfish misers of love, and therefore loveless.

How can we love our children so that they will become givers of love rather than hoarders of it? How can the freedom and power to love be released in them? The answer is, by encouraging their love responses. We have already recognized the importance, first, of the need to be loved, and second, of the need to love. We now face the importance of our being able to accept love and of encouraging the attempts of people, and especially of our children, to express their love. We might assume that it is easy to welcome their responses. Unfortunately, our expressions of love do not always please those to whom we make them. Because our love offerings are not appreciated and accepted, we may feel unloved and rejected. After repeated attempts to express our love successfully, and having been repeatedly rejected and discouraged, we may give up and turn our love in on ourselves.

A rose gardener told me of an instance that illustrates how difficult it is to accept some love offerings. He not only grew roses, but exhibited them as well. On one occasion, he had several blooms that he was nurturing for a coming show, one of which was being produced on a bush of his favorite variety. On the day before the exhibit his four-year-old son appeared before him with ecstatic face and with his prize rose clutched stemless in his hand, saying, "Look Daddy, what I brought you." It was obvious that the youngster, who adored his father, thought that he was presenting the perfect gift of his love, because he knew how much his father liked that particular rose. The father, on the other hand, confessed that he responded as the rose grower and exhibitor, rather than as one who had an opportunity to encourage his son's love responses by recognizing, from his son's point of view, the appropriateness of the gift. When, therefore, he very understandably scolded and spanked his child for picking the rose, the little boy was dreadfully upset. Episodes of this kind, if only occasional, are not serious, because they are experienced in the context of a relationship that is predominantly loving, supportive, and encouraging.

When the expressions of love and affection of children are not received with understanding and acceptance, their attempts to learn to love find no encouragement. Because they are being prevented from learning to love their parents and others, they are being prevented also from learning to love God in and through them. Our Lord's response to the gifts brought to Him demonstrates the kind of responses we should make to one another. Even when people's gifts were poorly motivated and ill-chosen, He was able to look behind them and see and understand the person who gave. Although Zacchaeus seemed to be motivated only by curiosity, our Lord invited him to come down out of the tree and asked that He might have dinner with him, thus moving behind the greed that had made Zacchaeus a publican.[1] And because our Lord was able to accept the gift of Mary Magdalene, her true love was called forth.[2] So it is with us. Our offerings often are pitiful and ill-chosen, but He looks upon the heart and sees there that really we are trying to express our love despite our ill-chosen means of doing so.

If we are to participate in the life of Christ and be the instruments of His love, we must learn to be hospitable to one another's efforts to express love. Parents need to look upon the hearts of their children and see deeply what they are trying to express. Husbands and wives likewise need to look behind the externals of behavior. What we do on the outside often fails to represent truly and adequately what is on the inside. We all need encouragement to love, and hospitality toward human attempts to express love is one of the surest ways in which we can participate in the contemporary living of Christ in the world.

Some Disciplines of Love

Now there are some disciplines that we need to follow as we engage in the dialogue of love. First, there is the discipline of giving oneself. It is the discipline of keeping oneself responsible for and to one another, responsible in facing issues and in making decisions. The only way to love is to communicate love by word and action. We may learn to use our power of being to speak and act the word of love. We should refuse to withhold it for any reason, including our fear of speaking it. Of course, there is risk in giving ourselves. Our gift of love may not be accepted, may not be appreciated, and may even be exploited. In giving love we may be hurt because of the nature of others' responses. But we will be stronger for having given it, and others may be called forth by it. Life cannot remain the same when love has been expressed.

[1] See Luke 19:2 ff.
[2] See Luke 7:37 ff.

Second, there is the discipline of holding ourselves to our own part. This is the discipline of allowing others to speak for themselves; or again, the discipline of refraining from trying to carry on both sides of a dialogue. We are always doing this; that is, we speak to the image we have of the other person. We try to anticipate his response and take away his freedom to respond and speak for himself. We choose our part of the dialogue in response to what we think his reaction will be and thereby rob ourselves of our freedom to be. There can be no communication between the images which two people hold of each other. Communication is possible only between two persons who, out of mutual respect, really address one another.

A third discipline is to accept the demand in love and our obligation to meet that demand. The compulsive element in love is hard for us to accept. But we cannot separate law from love. Law is implicit in love. Our Lord, Who is the incarnation of divine love, warned that He would not remove one bit of the law. He did not destroy the law, but by His love fulfilled it. It is really good that law is a part of love. Our own love relationships benefit from the presence of law in love, because law guides and protects our relationship. When we are "in love," or in union with one another, we are not conscious of the law, but it is implicitly present. We can be said to be "living above the law."

The law that is implicit in the relationship between a man and a woman who love each other is that they shall respect and act trustworthily in relation to one another; that they shall care for one another in all the ways that are necessary to their relationship. As long as love prevails, they are not conscious of this law. They do not need it. But if for any reason they should "fall out of" love, then they become conscious of their obligations to each other. Their relationship is now lived under the burden of law, and they will find it harder to observe than they did before. They now are being held together by their obligations, and it may be that while being thus held together they will again find each other in love. When they look back on this period some years later, they may call the whole experience love, because then they will see that the obligations of their relationship are a part of their love. Obviously, this is mature and not infantile love. Love that accepts responsibility and its obligations is love that is not primarily concerned about its privileges, although it gives thanks for whatever privileges it has. It recognizes itself not primarily as an emotion, but as a way of life; and it is more concerned about commitment than sensation.

By the employment of these principles that we have just rehearsed, we can help our children grow in their capacity to love and thereby become more capable of a heroic commitment to one another. This kind of commitment should characterize the members of the Christian fellowship, the men and women in whose lives the Spirit of the Christ is incarnate.

We have seen that we need to be loved in order that we may love others and that we should encourage one another's love responses. Does this mean that our attempts to express love should be accepted without correction? What should the rose-growing father of the little boy have done? One view is that the father should have accepted the gift with thanks, recognizing only the child's intention. Certainly, his intentions should be honored and his gift accepted. But the boy also needed help in learning how to express his love to others. Here is something we are always having to learn. All of us have had the experience of doing or giving something that was intended to be an expression of our love, only to discover that the gift was not appreciated by the one to whom it was given, and we find ourselves saying, "Oh, I didn't mean it to be that way." With children and with one another we need to strike a balance between acceptance of the intention and guidance in choosing the means for the expression of love. Loving is an art, and we all need to learn the art and to refine its practice. One would expect Christians and church people, who are supposed to be incarnations of the spirit of love, to be masters of the art. Yet, to the world, we often appear to be ungracious people. So let us learn to love one another, and let

us train our children in the practice of the art of love, by encouraging and disciplining them in it.

If a text for this responsibility were needed, we might take it
from the ancient liturgical language of the church in which we
say, "We receive this person into the congregation of Christ's
flock," which should mean that we receive the person into the
congregation of persons in whom the love of Christ is incarnate.

The Language of Words and Life

Unfortunately, however, we often use the words that suggest
the right meaning but fail to carry out that meaning in our lives.
All too easily our religious statements become empty forms, separated from the vitality and meaning which they are supposed
to express. Remember, for instance, how vainly we sometimes
say the Lord's Prayer, which is a form that our Lord gave us,
by means of which we could express the vitality of our relationship with God and one another. Likewise, we can honor and use
the correct verbal and other symbols about the church and Christian fellowship, its rites and ceremonies, and yet fail to translate
them into action, with the result that our rites and ceremonies
and doctrinal statements become dry, empty forms. Instead of
being the means of new life, they may only disappoint people,
because they do not really communicate the meaning that they
seem to promise. Every church should always test whether its
forms are really expressive of the truth which it professes. It is
not enough that we speak the truth; we must live it.

It has been given to men to communicate both by word and by
the life that is lived. There must always be a vital relation between the meaning that is being communicated in the word and
the form or means of its communication. The breakdown of
education and of religion occurs when there is a breakdown between the human experience with its meaning and the word
which represents it. This breakdown is complete when speaking
the word becomes a substitute for living its meaning. This breakdown also occurs when a culture undertakes to educate by means

of words and concepts only, and neglects to employ what happens between man and man as an integral and indispensable part of the curriculum.

The word and the meaning of the experience belong to each other and need each other, and the relation between them is a necessary part of education. Let us use the word "fight" as an illustration. We have this word because of man's experience in fighting. Out of the relationships of conflict and combat comes the experience we think of as fighting, and the word "fight" stands for it. The very young child learns to fight before he learns the word "fight." So far as he knows, the experience of fighting exists only between himself and his mother, and it is necessary for him to discover that fighting is a universal human activity. He learns the meaning of the word "fight" by the meanings that he brings out of his own combat, and on the basis of these he begins to understand the universal meaning of "fight." The word thus unites his little, individual experience with the experience of the human race of which he is a part. Therefore the word becomes an effective instrument in teaching him the meaning of his experience in the context of the experience of his own kind.

Similarly, because of his relationship to his mother, the child may experience her trustworthiness long before he knows the word "trust," but he needs a word for this experience. Then, as he begins to acquire the ability to convey these meanings with words, he learns the word "trust" and immediately the door opens so that his experience becomes related to the much larger experience of the people that have lived before him. If a child is being brought up in the Christian fellowship, the minute he begins to have a word to describe the trustworthiness of his relationship with his mother, he also begins to understand the meaning of trust as Christians have experienced it in relation to God.

On the other hand, it is difficult to convey the meaning of Christ's death to a child. Here the words are crucial to the understanding of the meaning, but he cannot bring out of his own life sufficient experiences to make the meaning of the concept available to him. But it is important to introduce him to these concepts by means of words against the time when the words will carry meaning. As we live with our children we help them interpret the meaning of their experiences. Some day they will be able to move from the little meanings that they have accumulated about life and death to the great meanings of the life and death and resurrection of Christ by means of the little word "cross" and other associated words. Education requires the use of both the language of words *and* the language of relationships. We teach children the words of our faith, but at the same time we try to live with them in ways that will provide the meanings that will prepare them for understanding the meanings of the faith. And this is what I mean when I suggest that what happens between us is an indispensable part of the curriculum.

The Curriculum of Relationship

This emphasis upon the relationship between parent and child, between teacher and pupil, between person and person, as a part of the learning situation, seems to put a heavy burden upon the teacher. After all, it was difficult enough when the teacher had to be responsible for the correct words for the transmission of the truth, and for the understandings that must go with them. Now, in addition, we have to pay attention to what is going on between teacher and pupil. The work of teaching is much bigger than mere verbal transmission, and nothing less is worthy of being called Christian teaching.

This kind of teaching requires that the truth being taught be incarnate in the relationship between men, which was what God did in Christ. The teaching of Christ is contained not only in His words, but also in His life. His life gave meaning to His words and made them uniquely different from any other words that had ever been spoken. Actually, many of the things that our Lord taught were not new, but His life was, and this made His teaching unique. The same principle must apply to us. Some instruction given in the name of Christian education is dull, monotonous, and irrelevant. There is nothing untrue about it, but it is taught without the conviction born of experience, and it is not expressed in what goes on between man and man. On the other hand, a recognition of the responsibilities of this kind of teaching should be coupled with the joys and satisfactions of it. It is the kind of teaching that can relieve us of some of the anxieties of accomplishment.

A Word of Encouragement

Many parents and teachers are concerned about the quality of the care and teaching which they give children, and they are particularly worried about their failures and sins in relation to them. Present in many of us is the fear that we may have permanently impaired the future welfare of those for whom we are responsible. This leads us to try to be perfect in the discharge of our duties and thus prevent serious injury to our children. In other words, we would like to love them perfectly, which, if we were able to do, would ill prepare them for their life in this world.

Furthermore, and more importantly, implicit in this anxiety is a grave misconception of what it means to be a Christian. The test of our love and faith is not the absence of failure and sin and problems, but lies in what we are able to do about them. Of course, Christian parents get angry with their children and say and do things that hurt them. We are haunted by the signs in our children that we have failed them, by the evidences of their anxiety, by the problems they sometimes have in relation to other people, by their lying and stealing, by their hostility and quarrelsomeness, and by their excessive competitiveness and jealousy. Sometimes the scenes around the family table are far different from our image of what Christian family life and fellowship should be. We wonder where we have failed, grow discouraged, and fail again. We are embarrassed by the contradiction that our children see between the things that we say and the things that we do.

Parents and teachers who, like Mrs. Strait, live by the law,

either have to blind themselves to what's going on in their relationships or else become profoundly discouraged. And if we
are like Mr. Churchill, our decision will be to ignore human problems and to turn ourselves to a devotion of God, as if that were
possible! Dr. Manby would wait for time to take care of the
matter, and Mr. Knowles would frantically cram more knowledge
about the Bible into the minds of parents and children in the
hope that, somehow or other, knowing about God and Christian
teaching would produce the necessary changes. Mr. Clarke, of
course, would turn the whole "mess" over to the clergy.

Implicit in the situations we have been discussing is a concept of success, the assumption being that if we love God and our
neighbor everything we do will turn out all right. My grand-
father always maintained that his business prospered because he
kept the laws of God. When we stop to think about it, we realize
what a faulty concept this is. After all, it was not easy for Christ
to accomplish the purposes of love in this world, and there is no
reason why it should be any easier for us. It is not easy to maintain the dialogue of life; it is not easy to call forth the being of
others; it is not easy to regain the freedom to love even when
we respond to the spirit of love. We recognize the credibility and
promise of all these principles, but wonder at the difficulty of their
application.

The Work of Love

We need to remember that even God, with all of His power
and wisdom, does not give His love to us in ways that take away
our freedom of response. He leaves us free to say Yes or No to
Him, to love, to our families, and to all the responsibilities of
life. This means, as we saw earlier, that we are to speak the word
of love and leave the other person free to make his response. We
cannot expect a guaranteed response from him. We cannot prevent him from making a wrong response any more than we can
make him give the right response. Our children are free, and
we must respect that freedom. This is why the achievement of a

love relationship is so exceedingly difficult. In the achievement
of any relationship we are involved in a life-and-death struggle.
Our children, for instance, want our love, care, and protection.
At the same time, they want to be their own selves and to assume
responsibility for their own lives. They can and do resent, with
devastating hostility, action on our part that looks to them like
interference with their lives. On the other hand, we love them
and feel that we cannot do enough for them. The effect of our
zeal often is to overwhelm them with our care and deprive them
of the freedom in which to achieve their power of being.

Inevitably, then, the living dialogue between the parent and
the child is both a happy and a troubled one in which the powers
of love and resentment are exerted on both sides. The struggle
between freedom and tyranny in human relations is understood
in the struggle of the cross, which takes place in every individual
and in every relationship. The actualization of ourselves in relation to one another is both difficult and painful. It is hard to
understand how anybody could ever think it was easy. The struggle calls for a love that is prepared to lay down its life for its
friends. The entrance of love into life brings, sometimes, not
peace but a sword. Tension and conflict may accompany the
work of love. The conflict between the love of God and the self-
centeredness of man produces an ugly, rugged, and bloody struggle, which the crucifixion summarized.

The Power of Love

The good news of the gospel is not that a way has been given
us by which to avoid conflict, but that the power of love has been
given us for the conflict. With it we can enter into the shambles
of life with assurance, courage, and a belief that, even though
we cannot always understand what is going on, the purpose of
love is to reunite man and man, and that in Christ God's love
won the initial victory in this process. We may, therefore, participate in the life of the world with all of its conflicts, including
our own personal conflicts, with faith in the power of reuniting

love. We should not be surprised when we find ourselves embroiled in conflict and involved in complex situations. Our faith is not in our ability to do right, but in the power of God to help us re-enter the difficult and unpleasant situations we have created with new hope and with healing love. We may be thankful that God revealed Himself through a cross and, therefore, made clear how realistic He is in relation to the characteristics and conditions of human existence.

The power of love is liberating. It frees us so that we can use what happens between us as a part of the curriculum of Christian living and learning. Instead of wasting our time worrying about why things happen, we can use our energies and our understandings to deal with them constructively. The purpose of Christianity is not alone the prevention of crime, but the redemption of criminals; not alone the prevention of sin, but the saving of sinners. The great Christian word is redemption, which means transforming a destructive relationship into one in which the conditions and purposes of love are realized. Let us remember that fine linen paper is made out of old dirty rags. Similarly, a wonderful Christian relationship can be formed out of one that seems tragic. As we have seen, the test of a man is not in what happens to him, but in what he does about what happens to him. The transformation of what happens in human relations is the work of the Holy Spirit, continuing the work that was begun in Christ. The Spirit gives the gift of reconciling love with which we may participate in the continuing work of Christ, which is the redemption and transformation of life. So in the context of this love we can relax while we also exercise our care.

Love and Sin

The power of love over sin is widely recognized. In the first place, there is no judgment like the judgment implicit in love. The face of love is compassionate, but it gives a light that reveals the darkness of our hearts. We know that we are judged, but we know also that we are not condemned. The judgment and the forgiveness come to us as a part of the communication of love. Have we not felt this as we stood in the presence of someone whose love was true? We wished to be rid of everything in us that was unworthy of that love. In that same instant there may have welled up within us a repentance and a determination to live in response to that purifying, reuniting love. Such is our experience when the Spirit of Christ brings us face to face with Him and His love. To be loved is to be illumined, purified, and transformed, because love has the power of re-creation.

Parents and others who are conscious of their failures and sins in relation to their loved ones should remember that human beings are fundamentally resilient and resourceful. Children's springs of life and vitality are powerful. Their need to affirm themselves as persons is undeniable, and any experience of love that they have is reinforcing. Experiences of unlove are to them unbelievable and point, fundamentally and finally, to the necessity and believability of love. While our children are dependent upon us for their personal environment in which to grow up, they bring powers and resources to their growing up which are independent of us. They bring something to the dialogue in which self-actualization occurs. Their part of the dialogue is just as important and indispensable as ours. We cannot live their lives for them. They have to live their own lives, and our part is to live in relation to them and contribute our assistance to their powers of becoming.

Parents and teachers are not the only ones who influence their children. We live in a society in which different people have different roles to play in relation to everyone else. We should not measure the progress of a child only by how we see him or by what we think he is receiving from us. Our impression of the child's progress may be mistaken. We may not be able to know him as he is, nor know what others are contributing. And, least of all, can we know the total effect of all his relationships on what he is becoming as a person. Our anxieties about a particular incident may exist because we fail to see it in its total context.

Much happens in the development of a person's life that we do not see, and much of the transformation occurs secretly at levels so deep that we cannot observe it. Although we may not see what is happening, we may be sure that something is. In the sphere of the personal we need to trust both God and man, and if we trust God we can trust man. We then may take a long view of our task, and teach and work and live by faith.

This is what it should mean to be a Christian and a member of the church of Christ. What a wonderful thing it is to belong to a fellowship that is made up of people who may be united by the Spirit of God and through whom we believe that God works! What a comfort it is to know that we do not have to do and believe everything ourselves! Not only do we not have to live and believe and love for ourselves, but others live and believe and love for us at times when we cannot. But let us also remember that we have to live and believe and love for them when weakness or doubt or hostility seems to overwhelm them. This is the meaning of Christian fellowship; namely, that we are not an aggregation of individuals, but instead are members of one body, with every member having his own function, and the function of every member standing in a complementary relation to that of the others, of which body Christ is the head. Here is the source of the love about which we have been speaking and the process through which love is lived in the life of the world that God loves.

IV

SOME OBJECTIVES OF LOVE

"Little children, let us not love in word or speech
but in deed and in truth."—*1 John 3:18*

THE OBJECTIVE OF LOVE, as we have seen, is to "move everything to everything else that is," especially to reunite person to
person. This is an identifying characteristic of the love of God,
and it is to some degree the characteristic of all love. We believe
that this love was incarnate in Jesus Christ. We believe that His
Spirit, active in the world in which we live, seeks to incarnate
this love in us here and now. Furthermore, we have identified
some more general characteristics of love. Now we turn to look
at some of the ways in which love accomplishes its purpose, a
purpose which is the responsibility of the church in its dispersion
in the life of the world.

Love's Sphere Is Personal

The sphere of love's action is in the realm of the personal; it
acts in and through relationships. The process by which the person emerges is both wonderful and fearful, and one for which we
should have reverence, the zeal to understand, and the willingness
to be responsible for. Certain specific things need to be accomplished which are the work of love, which we have already identified as the calling forth of persons. In this work of love we
participate in the reconciling work of God in Christ today. Let
us remember also that children first experience the love of God
through their experience of their parents' love, and that parents in
loving their children are loving God, since we love God by loving
one another. How else can we love God than by loving one an-

61

other? With this understanding of the context in which we live and work and serve one another, let us turn our attention to how love's task is accomplished.

First, however, a word about what that task is not. The objective of love is not to create or nurture a so-called normal human being. In the first place, there is no universal concept of the normal, and the criterion of normality varies from age to age and from culture to culture. All men have problems and always will have them. The pursuit of perfection is a perilous project that may cause all kinds of imperfections and will inevitably produce disillusionment.

Adjustment cannot be the goal of Christian living and the objective of love. The clam is adjusted about as well as any of God's creatures, but has very little to offer beyond a passive role in a bowl of soup. Instead of striving to mold a person completely adjusted to his surroundings, love seeks to nurture a person who is capable of maintaining a creative tension between his need and his responsibility, between the vitality of spirit and the form of being. And, according to tests, such creative people often are classified as not normal and not well adjusted.

Nor is the pursuit of happiness the objective of love. Happiness for human beings is a forlorn hope. Because of conflicts within himself and between himself and others, man is doomed to be unhappy most of the time. He is always having to deal with the inevitable conflicts and accidents of life that give him a sense of vulnerability, both as an individual and as a member of his tribe, nation, or race. Instead, the objective of love is to provide the human being with resources, by means of which he may face his human existence with courage and with a sense of peace that passes understanding. It now remains for us to spell this out in human terms.

Dialogue Between Individual and Environment

When the human being is born, he leaves the biological exchange of the womb for the social exchange system of his society, where his gradually increasing capacities meet the opportunities and limitations of his culture. The appearance of the person, therefore, results from the dialogue between himself and his environment, between his growing, autonomous self and the directing community upon which he is dependent. This dialogue between the individual and his environment often has, as we have seen, the characteristics of a conflict. The individual challenges and makes demands of his family, and the family challenges and makes demands of the child. Each wrestles with the problems of trust in relation to the other, each wrestles for autonomy that is equal to the domination of the other, each strives for the initiative and industriously competes with the other, and each seeks an identity that may either exclude or include the other. The quality of the life of the individual and of the social order depends upon the results of the dialogue between them.

I am thinking of two families. In one, the parents helped their children work through their difficulties with each other, thus assuming dialogical responsibility for what happened between them. In late teenhood, each child in turn became a person in his own right who had achieved a relatively mature, congenial, and loving relation with every other member of the family. In the second family, the parents could not face the conflicts inevitable to human nature in a growing family, and pretended a quality of relationship that did not exist between them. When their children became late teen-agers and older, a smoldering antagonism existed between them which occasionally broke out in venomous quarrels. The parents of this second family had not assumed dialogical responsibility for the content of their family life, with the result that the interaction between the growing person and his environment was not creative.

The process of unfolding patterns, of decisions made in response to crises, of frustrations and achievements in living, are also the human content for religious development, and provide opportunities for both conversion and nurture. The development of a person is religiously significant, and the events in his life have ultimate meaning. We may think of them in only psychological and sociological dimensions, but their meaning also is theological and religious. As we weave our intricate way through the years of our lives, approaching and withdrawing, attacking and retreating, victorious and beaten, decisive and uncertain, being loved and being resented, loving and hating, and sometimes gladly and sometimes reluctantly participating in the dialogue between ourselves and our environment of influential persons, we may ask ourselves this question: What contributes to our emergence as responsible, resourceful persons? As participants in the dialogue between our children and ourselves, for example, we should like to know the kind of address and response we should make that would call them forth as persons who will be responsible and helpful in relation to their dependents, peers, and superiors; and enable us, through them, to love and serve God. How can we so participate with them in living that there will be called forth in them a courage that will dare the risks of creativity and acquire the freedom to love?

The dialogue between the individual and life is initiated by the basic question that is implicit in our being, and becomes explicit as our capacities as persons increase. The basic question is: Who am I?, and associated with it is its partner question: Who are you? These two questions have to be asked together almost as if they were one question, because there is no answer to the question: Who am I?, except as there is an answer to the question: Who are you? And this twofold question is not only asked implicitly by the newborn baby, but explicitly by his parents, whose own dialogue with the baby involves asking and receiving answers to Who are you? and Who am I? because the relationship is one in which the child also may call forth the parent as a person.

This basic twofold question is one which we all continue to ask all through our lives in many different ways. We must not associate question-asking exclusively with verbalization. Obviously, the baby cannot ask his mother in words who she is. He does it by his actions, by his random movements, by his crying, by his protests, by his exploring hands and eyes, by his mouth. And the mother does not give reply to his question by word only, but by her actions; by her feeding and care of him, by her neglect, by her joy in him and her irritation because of him, by her coming to him and by her unexplained departures from him. All her actions are a language by which she tells her child who she is in response to the questions implicit in his actions. And her answer to him as to who she is gives him the beginning of an answer to his question as to who he is.

Thus, the dialogue between mother and child, which is largely nonverbal, tells him that his mother is one who in some ways loves him and in others does not, and tells him also that he is one who in some ways is loved and in other ways is not. Out of this interchange emerges his manner of response which may become his style of living and loving. But we need to remember that his characteristics as a person are not wholly determined by the action of his environment, because they also are determined by who he is within himself as a unique being. His inheritance provides him a given quality and capacity. Therefore, the dialogue is to be understood also as a dialogue between heredity and environment in which his experience of love releases his power of being.

Sense of Trust

The first objective of love to be accomplished out of the dialogue between the individual and the world is the awakening in him of a sense of basic trust. Trust toward oneself and toward others is acquired to some degree during the first year. I have discussed this at some length in an earlier book, *Man's Need and God's Action*,[1] and here, as well as there, I acknowledge my indebtedness to the work of Erik Erikson.[2] In this chapter I shall

[1] *Man's Need and God's Action*, Reuel L. Howe, The Seabury Press, Greenwich, Connecticut, 1953. Chapter V.

[2] *Growth and Crises of the Healthy Personality*, Erik H. Erikson. Pamphlet from *Problems of Infancy and Childhood*, Josiah Macy, Jr. Foundation, New York, 1950. Used by permission.

discuss the other senses that he identifies as necessary acquisitions of the growing personality.

Perhaps the greatest contribution to the achievement of basic trust is through the experience of being fed. The experience of being fed regularly and responsibly causes the child to respond with trust, and he learns to have faith long before he knows the word for it. Later, at the appropriate time he acquires the word "faith" to point to the meaning of his trust experiences. If, still later, he allows the words to take the place of the substance of his faith, they will become empty words. Responsible parents and teachers seek to combine the right word with their action so that the meaning of the child's experiences is correlated with the words for them. A mature correlation between word and experience is one in which the child has the experience of finding people both trustworthy and untrustworthy, and has been helped to deal with the untrustworthiness in the context of trust. His first experience, therefore, is a realistic one in which he is strengthened by his experiences of trust, and is not made too anxious by his experiences of the inevitable failures of his loved ones to take care of him perfectly.

The child's experience of trust and mistrust contains the first meanings for his Christian education. The care of the Divine Father is expressed in and through the care of his earthly parents. His response to the care of his earthly parents is his response to his Divine Father. This needs to be interpreted to the child as he grows up, so that he will accept and believe in the participating presence of God in human life. An obstacle in the way of this achievement occurs when people separate God from life and make Him a kind of absentee operator of the machine called the world. It then is necessary for the child to make a huge leap from his trust of his parents to faith in God. While we cannot equate parental action with divine action, nevertheless we can affirm that divine action takes place through human action. When such an affirmation is made and accepted as a part of the parents' faith and is interpreted to the child as he is able to receive it, he is helped to grow up with a religious understanding of life itself, rather than conceiving of religion as being merely a part of life. He will grow up with the idea that being trustworthy and trusting others has not only psychological and sociological meaning, but also theological meaning.

A sense of trust is basic, because without it the further development of the individual would not be possible. Its foundations are laid in the very first year of an individual's life. The act of taking from his mother not just food, but her ministrations, her companionship and friendliness, is the beginning of his emergence as an individual apart from his parents. As he becomes an individual person, he immediately begins to be a giver as well as a taker. Giving, as well as receiving, must become a part of the dialogical relation between two individuals, whether between a child and the parent, or between two adults. As soon as a child begins to become a giver, the parent must consent to be a receiver of that which the child has to give, and thus, again, is a relationship of basic trust established.

Without parental reception the child would not be affirmed as a giver, and would, out of his mistrust, become a compulsive taker, a result that is tragic not only psychologically and sociologically, but religiously as well. He will not be able to trust God; but because he needs to trust God, he will begin to create images of God in the context of which he will try to handle his existential problems. Thus, the foundations of a false religion may be laid in early childhood, and this false religion, as it matures, closes the person off from the truth of the gospel and keeps him from becoming an instrument of the gospel in relation to the whole world. The church is filled with people who do not really trust God, even though they publicly profess their faith in Him. These people, like Mr. Clarke, Mrs. Strait, and the others, live timidly.

We must not conclude that the establishment of basic trust concerns only infants. The balance between trust and mistrust is something that concerns us all our days, and the question is raised acutely again every time we face a change in the circumstances of our lives. I have observed that when people come together in a new group relationship, their basic questions, Who am I? and Who are you?, are reactivated. Significant communication between them does not take place until some relationship of trust is established on the basis of satisfactory answers. Our initial asking of these questions in infancy is, to some degree, repeated at subsequent times in our lives. They are repeated in times of marriage, bereavement, retirement, death, or in any personal crisis; and also when we face the threat of war or the possibility of interplanetary existence, or in any economic, social, or political crisis. Needed at these times of threat are relationships with sufficient power to enable us to participate in the dialogue out of which will come the answers to our questions. The objective of love is to provide the relationship of love for a world that, again and again, and in an infinite variety of ways, asks the basic questions: Who am I? and Who are you?

How wonderful it is to participate in the answer to the basic questions! Mothers, for instance, who tend to lose the sense of purpose in the minutiae of their responsibilities, could be helped to realize how profoundly important is the care they give their children. The way in which they feed and care for their families may be, if they opened themselves to the presence and action of God in human life, the means of their child's union with man and God.

As we try to meet the physical and emotional needs of children, and travel with them through the various crises of life in which we both participate, we may have the reassurance that we are doing a great work, the full meaning of which we may not be able to see at the moment. Furthermore, we may be reassured that we are participating in the work of God in the world and engaged in the true ministry of the church in the world. When there is this living that awakens and renews trust, the formal teaching and religious observances of the church both receive and give additional meaning.

Sense of Autonomy

The second objective of love is the achievement of a sense of autonomy. We said earlier that as the child begins to take that which is given to him, he begins to distinguish between himself and others, and thereby to become a separate person. In so doing, he begins to achieve some degree of autonomy as an independent person. This second task is made easier for him, if he is able to approach it with a sense of trust. The need for a sense of trust in the achievement of autonomy becomes apparent once we recognize what this second task involves. It introduces the child into a conflict of interests. On the one hand, he needs the constant care, supervision, and love of his parents; and on the other hand, he needs to assert his own will and stand over against his parents as a separate person. He both needs to be a part of the mother and distinct from her. The conflict between these needs increases as the individual becomes a person.

This process, however, often results in a warfare of unequal wills between the child and the parent. The child himself is capable of violent drives which frighten him and which he is unable to control; and the parent can be provoked to emotional responses that escape his control and are frightening. The relationship between them, therefore, may become one in which each is seeking to dominate and control the other. This pattern occurs in all relationships and is often observed in marriage, where, by various kinds of behavior, each partner seeks to control the other.

The muscular mechanism basic to the achievement of autonomy is the mechanism of holding on and letting go. By the employment of it, the individual begins to be aware of his powers as a separate person. Awareness of these powers and of the possibilities inherent in them precipitates the struggle between him and others. A child can be very pliable or very stubborn in his holding on or letting go, and it is not long before parents discover that they cannot make a child do something that he will not do. At this point, the parent's own maturity in the employment of the same mechanisms will determine how he will respond to the child's stubborn and often hostile efforts to achieve autonomy.

As people mature, the holding-on and letting-go tension is transferred from the muscular to the emotional and psychological. If adults have achieved a relaxed attitude, they will be able to provide the child with firmness, and at the same time allow him some freedom in determining his own action. An environment of freedom and authority will help him achieve a balance between love and hate, co-operation and willfulness. An early sense of trust, we see, is necessary for the development of autonomy. Without trust the child will not feel free to struggle, as he must, for its achievement. He will not feel free, because he does not have faith either in himself or in his world, in relation to which he must struggle.

The objective of love, therefore, is to provide a relationship of firmness and tolerance within which a child may become autonomous and acquire a sense of self-control, self-esteem, and relationship with others. Otherwise he may suffer loss of confidence in himself and become skeptical of others, a result which can be the fruit of either restrictive discipline or unstructured freedom.

The achievement of a sense of autonomy must always remain relative, and will vary from individual to individual. As we have seen, there is no fixed norm for human behavior, and the best sense of autonomy that anyone can possibly achieve is one in which there is a mixture of co-operation and willfulness, of love and hostility. We can only hope and pray that as we all mature our autonomy will be employed with creative good will, and that it will be capable of dealing with the results of our hostility and stubbornness.

Although our sense of autonomy appears during our second and third year of life, its further development depends upon our relationship with others. Furthermore, its employment has other arenas than that of family life. The dialogue from which autonomy grows moves out of family and into the neighborhood. It is quickened and disciplined by entrance into school, is heated and tempered by the development of social life, especially by the dialogue between the sexes when the need to surrender oneself to the other meets the needs of each to be oneself.

Finally, the autonomy of the individual is sure to be challenged by the complexities and organization of modern industrial society. More and more the individual is being caught in the intricacies of a process in which his sense of autonomy and initiative is violated. The problems of the social order are so massive that the interests of the individual often are sacrificed. Increasingly, people are unable to endure the frustrations caused by their social, political, and industrial environment, and develop neurotic responses in which their aggressions are turned in on themselves. The autonomy and initiative that once belonged to the individual have been transferred to the social order, with the result that instead of individuals receiving their direction from within, they now receive it from without, with the inevitable demand for conformity, in which the integrity of the individual is apt to be sacrificed. Every time he turns on his radio or television set, his autonomy is assaulted by all kinds of pressures.

This condition presents education and religion with peculiar challenges. In order to minister to the world, it is necessary that one participate in the life of the world and share its problems as did our Lord. But if we are to be the instrument of God's purpose in the work of the world, it will be necessary for us to have a sense of autonomy and a power of independence. This is what it means to be in the world but not of the world.

One of the objectives of love, therefore, is so to live with one another, especially with our children, that out of that relationship we may emerge with such a power of being as a person that we shall be able to face the complexities, pressures, deprivations, and dangers of modern life. Our aim is to help the child become a responsible participant in the crucial issues of life, and to preserve his integrity as a deciding person. The answer to his questions, Who am I? and Who are you?, will then be: I am what I will, and you are what you will; and our relationship is one of mutuality in which each will call forth the other. If the awakening of a sense of autonomy is an objective of love, it is also the objective of the church's life, its teaching, and its evangelistic endeavor. Without power of autonomy and independence, Christians will be mere conformists and maintainers of the *status quo*.

Sense of Initiative

The third objective of love is to help the individual achieve a sense of initiative. At the age of four or five, a child is faced with his next crisis and must take his next big step. He must find out what kind of person he is going to be. His search will be strengthened by his experience of trust, and by whatever power of autonomy he has. Dr. Erikson points out that he wants to be like his parents who seem very wonderful to him, but who, at the same time, present him with very real threats. During this age he plays at being his parents. According to Dr. Erikson, there are three strong developments which help him, but which also contribute to his crisis. "First, he learns to move around more freely and more violently, and therefore establishes a wider, and so it seems to him, an unlimited radius of goals. Two, his sense of language becomes perfected to the point where he understands and can ask about many things just enough to misunderstand them thoroughly; and three, both language and locomotion permit him to expand his imagination over so many things that he cannot avoid frightening himself with what he himself has dreamed and thought up. Nevertheless, out of all this he must emerge with a sense of unbroken initiative as a basis for a high, and yet realistic, sense of ambition and independence." [1]

Initiative is the power that moves the individual to take over the role of others; the boy, his father; the girl, her mother; later as the driver of the car, and later still, leadership roles of various kinds. The struggles in the process are accompanied by feelings of anxiety, of inadequacy, and of guilt. Feelings of inadequacy in relation to the size and powers of the adult can be considerable; and the feelings of guilt, in response to the daydreams about re-

[1] Ibid.

placing Daddy, for instance, are crucial, and too often are un-recognized by many parents and teachers. They need to recognize and accept the developmental reasons for the child's preoccupations and fantasies about himself in relation to them and their roles and functions. Furthermore, it is entirely appropriate for him to be physically aggressive toward others, to overwhelm them with his incessant chattering, his aggressive getting into things, and his insatiable curiosity about everything. The objective of love at this time is to provide the child with a reasonable freedom within which to develop his initiative with a minimum sense of guilt in relation to its exercise, and with the hope that by so doing he will become a person whose creativity will not be frustrated by an overdeveloped sense of guilt.

In contrast, many people are embarrassed by recognition of their achievements, and are prevented from achievement because of guilt feelings that block their creative efforts. Unfortunately, too much religious teaching has made people feel guilty about initiative and aggressiveness, both of which can be expressed creatively. From childhood on, lives are hedged about by prohibitions in relation to persons bearing authority, by belittling attitudes toward themselves and toward their drives to compete and to get ahead, so that people become self-restricted and are kept from living up to their inner capacities or from using their powers of imagination and feeling. While some withdraw into a dull kind of existence, others overcompensate in a great show of tireless initiative and a quality of "go-at-it-iveness" at all costs. These people often overdo to a point where they can never relax, and they feel that their worth as people consists entirely in what they are doing rather than in what they are.

The objective of love is to help the child accept the necessary structures, authorities, and personal roles in relation to which he must live, so that he may grow in his capacity to love persons and to use things. During this stage of life, children often turn to other adults for companionship and guidance. They do so because the conflicts between themselves and these new adults do not seem to be as great as with their own parents. They need these "fresh" relationships where they can exercise initiative without too much conflict and guilt. Here the school and church, with its trained teachers and workers, have an opportunity to supplement, and even to correct, the experiences that children are having at home. We should remember, however, that the identifications with the parent are important, and that the experiences the youngsters are having with others should be of a complementary nature, even if they also are corrective.

Another and supplementary objective of love is the provision of a relationship by parents or others in which a spirit of equality makes possible an experience of doing things together, instead of a relationship in which the child has to compete unequally with the adult. Fathers, for instance, may be of great help to their sons. Boys are apt to feel that their fathers are too big, too powerful, and too skillful; but if the father will base the relationship on some interest or experience common to them both, the boy has an opportunity to grow in initiative and to develop his capacities without a sense of unequal competition.

The answer to the child's questions, Who am I? and Who are you?, will then be: I am what I conceive myself to be, and you are what I conceive you to be according to my understanding of how you have revealed yourself. At this particular time in the development of the individual, there begin to be formed the powerful images of ourselves and others that aid or hinder our relationship with one another.

Sense of Industry

A fourth objective of love is to help the individual to a sense of industry, for the child has now become a busy little person who needs to learn how to be busy with things and persons. A child's "busyness" begins with his play. Children play separately at first. In their youngest years, they may sit apart in the same room, each playing with his own things, and each oblivious of the other except when one may discover that the other has something he wants. Later, as they grow and mature, there begins what we call parallel play. They play along side of each other. Now they are aware of each other, and each keeps an eye on his playmate. Their separate playing seems to have an influence on the other in that they imitate each other. Then, at a still later stage, they begin to play together. The high point of this achievement, still later, is team play, which begins in adolescence or even earlier.

Now begins the capacity for directed fellowship. The fellowship of a team is to be respected. Membership on the team may mean more to the boy than membership in his church, and this may cause ministers, parents, and teachers considerable anxiety. Instead, they should relax and be glad for the youngster's experience, because team play is providing him with an experience of relationship that later will become the basis for his understanding of the ultimate meaning of all relationships. They should accept the youngster's experience and use it creatively, to help him understand the nature of the church, our relationship as brothers, and the "captaincy" of Christ.

In team play, also, we see the occurrence of something that is very much a part of Christian character. In order for there to be team play, it is necessary for every member of the team to die to the desire in him to be the whole show. A mature team member has learned that his strength and skills depend on the strength and skills of others. This is the theology of the playground. What has been learned in play may be translated into work. Then, since a man's work is one of the great spheres in which he may exercise his ministry as a representative of Christ, the learning of this profound lesson in the process of play is an important part of his religious education. And it can be religious, even though it may not be learned in the formal church.

The transition from play to work takes place gradually. Children become dissatisfied with play and make-believe, and have a growing need to be useful, to make things well, and, therefore, to acquire a sense of industry. They also learn to win recognition by producing things. Through play they advance to new stages of real mastery in the use of toys and things, and learn to master experience by meditation, experimenting, and planning. The home, the school, and the church should try to help them to make this transition easily in order that they may develop this sense of industry without a sense of inadequacy. If they are pushed too strenuously to produce, a sense of inadequacy may result, especially when they still want to be cuddled and cared for. Family life has the responsibility of preparing the youngsters for school, where, in the context of their play experiences, they accept the disciplines of work. Relaxed teachers are needed who understand the process by which children learn to move from play to work, and who can encourage them to make this transition without either sparing them the needed disciplines or imposing them too strenuously. Here we see an area in which the role of the family and the role of the school are complementary.

The acquisition of a sense of industry is a decisive step in learning to do things with others and alongside others. This will become a major source of satisfaction and the area of his greatest service.

Sense of Identity

A fifth objective of love is to nurture in the human being a sense of identity which is acquired and consolidated in a new way during adolescence. Dr. Erikson describes identity as the "accrued confidence that one's ability to maintain inner sameness and continuity is matched by the sameness and continuity of one's meaning for others." [1]

As an individual develops and acquires skills, he thinks of himself as one who can do things, and his important people may hold a variety of expectations of him: "He's clumsy," "He never can do anything right"; or, "I can always count on him," "He's got the right stuff in him." Out of his achievements and the attitudes of others toward him, his sense of self-esteem and prestige is built, little by little. As crisis after crisis is passed and the in-

[1] Ibid.

dividual meets each of them with reasonable resourcefulness and receives the encouragement and recognition of others, he begins to believe in himself, to have a consistent expectation of what he will do in the face of various circumstances and relationships. In this way he begins to acquire a style of living which is his own and which contributes to his sense of identity and to others' identification of him.

In the achievement of a sense of self-identity, the child needs models with which to identify himself. Especially is this true during his adolescence. He needs association with men who are clear about being men, and women who are clear about being women, and who are capable of and practice a reasonably wholesome relationship with each other. He needs men and women who have convictions, who can distinguish between right and wrong, who hold these convictions firmly, and yet not rigidly. He needs guides and counselors who can help him bring together and concentrate his various and fluctuating drives and interests, and who are not dismayed or misled by the inconsistencies and fluctuations that may accompany his development. He needs help in choosing a job, because self-identification is dependent upon some kind of occupational identity. Finally, he needs help in acquiring, as a part of his sense of self-identity, a sense of vocation, of being called to something that is greater than himself, which will draw him forth as a participant in the deepest meaning of life. The providing of this kind of relationship to help the individual acquire an indispensable sense of identity is another of love's objectives.

Unfortunately, however, in our complex and technical society, the models after which the youngsters may now pattern themselves are not as clear as they might be. People are having to undergo tremendous adjustments in a time of rapid technical growth, as a result of which their image of the world in which they live is changing; producing, therefore, uncertainties in themselves, and making it more difficult for adolescents. Our changing age creates many difficulties for changing adolescents. Cultural conditions often force young people to band together in groups or movements that provide them with a point of focus by means of which they stereotype themselves and their ideals. This is one way in which they acquire stability and a sense of direction. We need, however, to be tolerant of this and to recognize its purpose; we need to realize also that if we provide them with alternatives, their need for these stereotypes may disappear.

The church has a special role here. Most of the committee whose discussion we read in Chapter I, gave no evidence of being able to provide young people with the kind of models they need, for there was nothing heroic, clear-cut, or creative about them. Their faith was defensive, and it did not deal with the realities of life. Young people turn away from that kind of "religion." And quite rightly. They need men and women whose religion, instead of being a defense against life, provides them with the courage to move into life and become a part of it, to accept its problems and wrestle honestly for its meanings; whose style of Christian living is not compulsive, but liberated; not pretentious, but honest; whose reverence for God is not confined to the sanctuary, but is exhibited in responsible relations with people. They need models who, because of their religious faith, are able to admit when they are wrong and can ask for forgiveness without feeling a loss of personal dignity. They need religious teachers who can portray, both by word and by example, the great personalities of the tradition, the heroes and saints; teachers who are clear about what their contribution really is, who can make clear to youth the heroism of a man of faith and let it stand forth without all the confusions of superstitious veneration. They need a church and religious teachers and members that have a sense of mission, a reason and purpose for living that is related to all the exciting meanings of human life, instead of being concerned with such irrelevancies as churchism, parochialism, institutionalism, and other modern idols. In the context of this kind of example, adolescents, even in complex, modern, industrial America with all its confused values, will have the aid they need in order to move through the intricacies of their development and emerge with a sense of personal identity and a capacity for relationship.

Sense of Integrity

A final objective of love is to help the individual, who by now has become an adolescent and is fast approaching the threshold of adult life, to achieve a sense of integrity. The acquisition of the senses of trust, autonomy, initiative, industry, and identity through the years of his development should prepare him for responsible living with himself and others. Much depends, as we have seen, on the ability and willingness of those in his environment to accept, respond to, and guide him. But there is still unfinished business with which we must help him; namely, the achievement of a sense of integrity.

A sense of integrity includes a capacity for intimacy with others. More than sexual intimacy is meant, although that is of more importance than many religious people want to admit. For the moment, however, we are thinking of intimacy in a general sense, of our capacity to participate in the meanings of one another's lives, to fuse into relationships without losing our respective identities. We see young people striving to achieve this kind of relation with each other through their talking things over endlessly, by confessing what one feels like and what the other seems like, and by sharing dreams, ideals, and ambitions. Where this is not achieved by early adulthood, the individual may find himself separated from others except for formal and stereotyped interpersonal relations.

Only the person who is capable of intimacy can become a partner in any relationship. People who marry with the hope of achieving the power of intimacy are often disappointed, because mutually fulfilling sexual intimacy requires a capacity for personal intimacy. What we are trying to say here is that before one can become a partner, one must first be a person. With this we have reached a kind of summary in the development of our thesis which might be stated as follows: A person is called into being out of relationship, but the person in his separateness is necessary to the achievement of a new relationship.

Intimacy is not only platonic, but sexual as well. The growing person needs help in acquiring a potential capacity for mutual, satisfying intimacy with a partner of the opposite sex. Heterosexual mutuality has religious significance, since sexual intimacy is supposed to be an outward and visible sign of personal intimacy. Yet religion is often strangely silent in this area, and our young people are often misled. A teen-ager recently said, "I don't go much for this platonic stuff." When asked why, he said, "I guess I'm too much of a wolf." When asked what he meant by being a wolf, he said that he was interested only in making love to a girl. His view of intimacy, which is similar to that of many other young people, reveals at least two misunderstandings: first, the separation in his mind between the platonic kind of relationship and the sexual, and secondly, his association of the sexual with "wolf," which is a symbol of the subhuman. Religious teaching needs to affirm sexual intimacy as a part of people's lives, and nurture them so that their sexual relationships may be a means of grace rather than a source of guilt.

The achievement of intimacy, general and specific, leads to the development of another capacity essential to integrity; namely, the capacity for generation, whether of offspring or creativity of some other kind. Generative capacity is basic to an individual's assumption of responsibility, and to his ability to initiate and bring to fulfillment new life or new expressions of life. The power of origination is open to anyone, and we can either affirm the power or deny it. If we deny it, we shall have to find substitutes which usually are subpersonal and which involve us in a kind of superficial but unfulfilling intimacy. On the other hand, the person with integrity is one who can initiate creativity of his own, or consent to and participate in the creativity of others. As Dr. Erikson has pointed out, he can be both a leader and a follower. These are qualities and values needed by all men, and the cultivation of them is the task of the church and the purpose of its teaching.

The objectives of love, we see, are not abstract, but specific and concrete. Love calls forth persons and reunites life with life by providing the relationships in which the created needs of men are met. The environment of saving love is needed to produce out of our biological nature and the physical world in which we live the image of God in each of us and the Kingdom of God for all of us.

V

THOSE WHO WOULD LOVE

"We know that we have passed out of death into life,
because we love the brethren."—*1 John 3:14*

THUS FAR IN OUR DISCUSSION we have considered the nature
of love, the development of the needs of the individual, and the
objectives of love in calling persons into being. Now we turn to
a discussion of the lover, or of the person or persons who are the
instruments of that love, such as parents, teachers, ministers, and
every man of whatever function. We shall also consider the
nature of the relationship in which healing and reconciliation
take place, and consider some of its resources.

The Power of the Personal

The doctrine of the Incarnation, which underlies the whole
Christian life, is really the doctrine of the personalization of love.
By it is meant the embodiment in man of the life of God Who
is love. The Incarnation makes this life personal, and persons,
therefore, are of primary importance to its existence and its meaning. In each generation the Christian is called upon to reaffirm
his faith in the power of persons living in relation to God and
man.

Our own generation has a special need for a reaffirmation of
the personal because of our preoccupation with science and tech-
nology, and with vast space and enormous power. One wonders,
and hears others wondering, what good is a person in the face
of all these masses, spaces, and complexities. But it was revealed
in Christ, and every now and then it is revealed to us afresh, that
the whole vast structure of life is dependent upon the power of

persons and upon our exercise of the power of the personal. The character of man, expressed in his relations with his fellow man, will finally determine whether we will use our vast powers creatively or for our destruction.

The primary vocation of the Christian in this time is to respond to the call of the person to be personal. The church members with whose conversation we began this book, seemed oblivious to the personal nature of the church's purpose. They were concerned about substitutes for the personal, about institutions and professional groups, about a legalistic morality, and about knowledge for its own sake. Any one of their concerns, if caught up in the vitality of the personal, could have valuable meaning. Law, as we have seen, has its role, if it is a part of love. Human effort is important as personal response to what God has done for us. Dependence upon the clergy is a part of the life of the church, but the work of the clergy, as we have seen, cannot be a substitute for the ministry of the whole church. The church is important, but it does not find its meaning in its isolation from the world. And knowledge about God, His creation, and redemption is necessary to the Christian life, but such knowledge must find its meaning in our living relation with God.

The recent emphasis on the interpersonal and group process has contributed much to our understandings of the human relationships of Christian fellowship. As a result of the emphasis, a new polarity operates in the life and teaching of the church: one pole is the content of the Good News; the other pole is the encounter between men in which the Good News is realized. Unfortunately, the image of the relationship between the encounter and the content of the Christian faith has been and still is that of opponents in a battle. This concept is erroneous, for any dialogue must have content. The conversation between two people that is not informed by learning produces nonsense. Discussion groups have revealed their poverty when they have not been informed by responsible knowledge; fellowship for the sake of fellowship becomes tiresome; and relationship without good discipline, whether in the home or elsewhere, becomes chaos and anarchy. So, there are some disciplines that we need to observe as persons in whom the Spirit of God seeks to incarnate His love.

We Need Informed Christians

First, if we are to embody and express the love of Christ in our generation, we must keep our minds alert and our interests alive. At this point, church people fail in several ways. Instead of having minds that search for the meaning of life in Christian terms, they sometimes have minds filled with musty opinions and prejudices. An otherwise alert lawyer, for example, said that he did not want his church to take a stand on any of the great social issues, but stick to its subject, namely, religion. This preoccupation with the subject matter of religion apart from its relevance to life is a characteristic failure of many church people.

As Christian churchmen, we do not need to be scholars in religion, but we should be interested in the issues of life, open to new understandings, and engaged in some kind of reading or study that will keep us informed and intellectually awake. Only in this way can we keep ourselves from falling into narrow little ruts and pulling the world in after us. A part of our ministry is to participate in and help to keep alive the dialogue between man and man, between the church and the world, between Christian thought and the problems of existence. Emotional and opinionated thinking about religion, values, and social issues is appallingly prevalent among "religious" people. The conversations of church members often are pitiful in their concern for the trivial affairs of the local church and institution, about its building and organizations, its suppers and bazaars. What a pathetic and inconsequential way of serving Christ! He needs, instead, men and women who are out on the frontiers of modern life, representing His message to the world.

The accomplishment of an intellectually and socially responsible ministry calls for some effort on the part of the local church. In the first place, the minister will have to preach, and teach out of, the gospel in its relation to life. Instead of talking so much about religion as an end in itself, he ought to talk about life in the context of the teaching of religion. The content of his sermons and instructions should be the affairs of men, for these raise the questions for which the gospel was given. The discussion of religion apart from life produces a laity who, in their life in the world, are unable to represent the message of the gospel, because they do not know that the message of the gospel has any relation to the affairs of life. Then we hear such laymen say to any minister who might try to speak relevantly to human questions: "Stick to your subject; I don't think these things are the business of the church."

Church members, as a part of their devotion to Christ who had love for the world, should try to understand the life of the world in terms of its deepest meanings, and not be content with merely its superficial values. They will read articles and books and editorials, and listen to speeches and forums on television and radio, not only that they may be informed, but also that they may be informed for God and may serve Him better in the world. Religion that seeks escape from the world, and similarly the person who will not assume responsibility for God in the world, is sinful and idolatrous. Protection against this sin and idolatry is partly secured by serving God with our minds and our interests.

Prayer and the Life of Devotion

A second discipline of the responsible Christian is the discipline of prayer and devotion. We cannot live in relation to God and serve Him if we do not communicate with Him. Prayer is one of the indispensable forms of the dialogue between man and man, man and God, and God and the world. Unfortunately, however, many people, including some clergymen, have given up prayer, because it seems unrealistic and unfruitful in this scientific age. A part of our trouble may be that we tend to separate our acts of prayer from our life of devotion. Or, to use a concept we have employed earlier, we separate the forms of prayers from the vitality which provides the life of devotion. Both public and private prayer lose their vitality by this separation of form from life, and by the separation of God from the world, so that we make Him the monarch of religion instead of the creator and redeemer of life. Because of our belief in love as God's chosen relation to the world and in the incarnation of love in the personal, it becomes possible for our prayers and worship to be quickened through our devotion to the purposes of God in the world.

An analogy may help us here. Every relationship has its devotional rituals and observances which are important to it. Husband and wife, for instance, because of their love and devotion to each other, develop little rituals and ways of doing that are designed to express their devotion to each other. They come together for this purpose. There is the kiss, the touch of the hand, the gifts on special occasions and those which come as surprises; their physical union is the symbol and instrument of their spiritual union and becomes the sacrament of their relationship as persons. But these acts of love presuppose and depend upon their over-all and lifelong devotion to each other in everything that they do. Their life of devotion to each other provides the content and drive for their acts of devotion, and their acts of devotion are a means of expressing their life of devotion. Their life of devotion needs these acts of devotion, and without the life of devotion their acts of devotion will dry up and become meaningless.

So it is in our relation to God. We cannot fall on our knees and cry with any meaning: "O God, O Father, O Judge, O Savior," if our whole lives are not lived in the context of the meaning of these exclamations. Then our words become empty and cannot rise above our lips, and we are overcome by the despair and futility of our prayers. Prayer may not be recovered by going to a school of prayer to learn various techniques and kinds of prayer, but by rekindling our devotion to the people and the world for whom Christ died. Then, by practicing our acts of

devotion in the context of such a life of devotion, we may redis-
cover the meaning of prayer. Our acts of devotion cannot be
quickened by the intensification of our prayer activity alone. Many
people who are frantically trying to whip up their prayer life
would do better to get up off their knees and go out and do
something about their loveless, purposeless, and undevoted lives.
The devotion of the so-called "children of darkness" to the
pursuit of their scientific or industrial purposes may be more
impressive than the vain babblings of the so-called "children of
God" about their souls. The trivial concerns of some religious
people stand in uncomplimentary contrast to the heroism of the
researcher's devotion to his project and to the scientist's devotion
to his experiment. Perhaps the purposes of God are more served
by them than by us, although by them His purposes may not be
served consciously.

How can the life of devotion and the acts of devotion be
brought together? When employer and labor leader meet to work
out the problems of fair employment, they may do so either as
a necessary part of their business, which of course it is, or as a
way of expressing their devotion to God. God's love is concerned
with justice between employer and employee, and the employer
and the labor leader participate in the work of God in the world
by their devotion to these problems. This is both their way of
being responsible businessmen and citizens, and their way of loving God and assuming responsibility for Him. To whatever
degree they recognize this as being true, they will find satisfaction
and meaning in the offering of their effort as an act of reverence
to God, together with a private prayer for His guidance that each
may be open not only to what God is trying to do through him,
but open also to what He is trying to do through the other.

In our acts of devotion, therefore, we pray for a life of devotion
in which we may be the instruments of God's purposes in the
incarnations of His Spirit. We pray also for others, for our
children, for our pupils, for our associates, whether they be employees, peers or superiors, that they too may be incarnations of

God's Spirit and instruments for the accomplishment of His purpose.

Acts of devotion, in the context of this kind of life of devotion, change the whole focus of human relations and get them off their self-centered, competitive, and alienating basis. Acts of devotion are revitalized by being restored to a relation to the life of devotion, and the life of devotion is given an opportunity in acts of devotion to articulate its meaning, and to be guided and renewed in the dialogue between God and man as expressed in worship. And the union of the acts of devotion with the life of devotion will illumine anew for us the meaning of daily life, and our relationships with one another. It will improve our dialogue with one another and with God.

The Practice of Creativity

A third discipline to be practiced by the person through whom the Spirit would work is the cultivation of creative activity. By the discipline of creativity, I mean the discipline of learning and perfecting some skill in art or music or handicraft or sport in which there is opportunity to co-ordinate motor and mental powers and to gain therefrom some sense of achievement. A creative approach to life, of course, is a part of a life of devotion. Creative activity is indispensable to the health of the human soul, especially in this day when there is an increasing gap between our efforts and their result.

Mothers are often frustrated and unhappy because they do not see immediately in their children the good results of their long and painful efforts in their behalf. Teachers can work with a pupil for months and years and still not have a clear-cut sense of achievement. The man in his office may be but a part of a huge organization, and the results of his labors are neither conclusive nor a source of immediate satisfaction to him. The researcher may have to work for years before he achieves the results for which he is looking. Indeed, he may never gain them for himself, because the work that he does may only lead to the work of others, and still others will reap the harvest. Then there are many engaged in work from which little sense of achievement can be gained, and yet it is necessary work and provides them with a living. Lack of response or delayed response to human effort can be profoundly frustrating to the human spirit, and frustrated people do not make good instruments for the expression of love. It is imperative, therefore, that those who would be lovers of man and God should find substitute ways in which to close the gap between their effort and their achievement.

The person who has a sense of creative outlets is one, therefore, who has greater powers of endurance, patience, and courage with which to face the challenges and threats of life. He is apt to be more free to love, and he will grow old more gracefully.

The discipline of creative action needs to be planned, time needs to be allowed for it, and those activities chosen which are feasible and appropriate to the person and his circumstances. We can learn to plan ahead so that from time to time we are prepared to undertake new projects. An elderly person of the writer's acquaintance began, during his sixties, to learn something new each year. The result was that his spirit remained youthful and his interest in life was kept alive. Not only is this kind of activity fun, but also it is a way by which to keep oneself open to the possibilities of life. It becomes a way in which one can live devotionally and realize within himself and in his relations with others the image of the creative God by Whom he was created.

Relationship as Resource

We come now to a consideration of the quality of relationship that nurtures persons. We discussed this earlier from the point of view of the child's need to be loved, his need to love, and his need to have his efforts to love welcomed. But now we turn to a discussion of relationship as a resource from the point of view of the one who is giving the love. We are thinking of the parent, the teacher, the pastor, or any other person who makes himself responsible for others.

It is curious how little we think of our relationship with one another as a resource. When someone comes to us who is in trouble, we often say, "I wish I could think of something to do or say that would help him," not realizing that the greatest thing we can do is to be a person in relation to him. Here again we realize the meaning of the incarnation. Everyone who hopes to participate in the life of Christ in the world today is called to be a person in relation to others, and whatever he thinks to do or say should be an expression of what he is.

If we say or do something that is helpful to others, it is because we are really present to them, really hear what they are trying to say, and they know that we are with them. On the other hand, we all have had the experience, when we were in trouble and needed help, of having would-be advisers and comforters make all kinds of suggestions and verbalize all kinds of would-be comforting thoughts, but have lacked the feeling that they were really with us. I sometimes have the impression that we like the idea of being helpful persons, but dislike the demand and disturbance that goes with it. It is easier to be depersonalized and professional, but professionalism is the enemy of relationship.

Professionalism is the conduct of a relationship for its own sake or for the sake of the "helping" person who is conducting it, rather than for the one for whom it was intended. Physicians, for instance, exhibit professionalism when they practice medicine without concern for the patient. Teachers exhibit professionalism when they teach their subject as an end in itself or for their own satisfaction. Ministers can be professional in relation to their parishioners. Parents can be professional in relation to their children. Any relationship can deteriorate into mere professionalism.

What are some of the marks of professionalism? In the first place, professionalism is marked by condescension in which an attitude of superiority is evident. Parents are heard to say: "Children are just children, you know. They don't know what they want; they don't know what they're talking about." Attitudes of condescension are contradictory to the concept of incarnation, which means to be a part of and identified with another. Condescension, therefore, closes us to the possibility of being indwelt by the Spirit and from being the instruments of love.

Another mark of professionalism is its manipulative tendency. We push people around and get them to do what we want them to do, because it is easier that way. "Mother knows best," "You do it because I tell you." Obviously, the professional attitude is alienating, because people do not like to be pushed around, and they will not be, if they can help it; and if they are, they resent it. Professionalism impoverishes relationship because, for instance, neither the parent nor the child gives or receives. The effect of professionalism does not need to be spelled out in any greater detail, because we all have experienced and participated in it. We may more usefully turn our attention to a study of the character of relationship that is the source of life.

The Values of Mutuality

Personal growth is nurtured best in relationships in which the quality of mutuality makes growth a possibility for both the child and the parent, the pupil and the teacher. If growth occurs on one side, it must take place also on the other. If parent or teacher does not grow, then we must conclude that the relationship is not mutual and that the child will not prosper either. Mutuality means that the teacher and pupil, or parent and child, are open to each other. When one speaks, he expects to be heard by the other.

Communication inevitably takes place in a relationship of mutual expectancy. Communication produces a personal encounter in which one addresses and the other responds, and a real meeting occurs. We cannot make this kind of personal meeting take place. We can only prepare ourselves for it, which is one way of thinking of prayer. When we practice expectancy in our relationships, we are preparing ourselves for possible depth meetings that may take place between others and ourselves. Preparation means ridding ourselves of prejudices and preconceptions, fears and anxieties, ulterior motives and purposes, in order that we may speak the word of love and truth to others, and really hear the word of love and truth that they speak to us. In similar fashion, we may prepare ourselves to be open to whatever God may speak to us through persons or situations during that day. Finally, because we have thus prepared ourselves for a real meeting between people, we will not so easily seek to manipulate and exploit them.

Mutual Attention

The quality of mutuality calls for mutual attention. Those who would call each other into being and be the instrument of God's love in human relations must pay attention to each other. It is difficult to speak if we do not have the listener's attention; it is difficult to listen if we do not have the speaker's attention. Absence of mutual attention breaks down communication. Sermons may not have the attention of the congregation because the preacher's attention is fixed only on the sermon as a production, or on himself as a performer, and not on the congregation that he is now addressing, and whose response is necessary if his sermon, as communication, is to be completed. Likewise, a child may not hear the parent because the parent is not really paying attention to the child. We hear ourselves saying, "Look here, you pay attention to me." We say it in desperation because we know that our angry command will not accomplish the desired result. The inattention that we receive from one another discourages us personally and blocks the possibility of the dialogue that might reunite us.

How can we secure the attention of others? The answer is simple: by being attentive. As a teacher I have found that if I am really attentive to my pupils, they pay attention to me. But if I am just doing a job and not really concerned about them, they do not hear me because I am not hearing them. If we want attention we must be attentive. If we want love we must love. If we want anything we must give it. This is a Christian principle.

We cannot demand something and get it. Attention, then, is a gift that we give one another. We give the gift of attention and receive it in return. We have no automatic right to it, nor does anyone.

Attentiveness is something that can be learned. We learn by having eyes that see and ears that hear. Eyes, of course, are made for seeing and ears for hearing, but we can learn also to hear with our eyes and see with our ears. When I am seeking to understand another, for example, I find that what I see in his face and manner helps me to understand what he is saying; and, likewise, attentive hearing helps me to understand what he is also revealing in his face and manner. We pay attention by watching the eyes, facial expressions, and behavior of people, by listening for the question behind the question and for the meaning behind the meaning, remembering that there is tremendous content behind what is said and shown. If we would be servants of love, we must have ears that really hear and eyes that really see; and, like our Lord, hear and see deeply in order that the truth which men are really seeking may be found. Such hearing and seeing was the gift of Christ to men, and should therefore be the gift of Christians to men.

It follows, then, that the good teacher is one who, participating in a relationship with our Master Teacher, can accept any question that a person may bring, knowing that if he stays with it, he will be led, step by step, to that person's real concern. When the teacher gives that kind of attention, the students are more apt to respond relevantly, which is their attention to the teacher. Then the teacher has the wonderful experience of mutual attention in which meaningful communication has taken place. What I have said about teaching and the relationship between teacher and pupil is true of all relationships. The reward for the gift of attention is that others will respond with clues in the form of questions or comments that will enable us to meet them at the point of the meaning of their life. Not only does this kind of listening provide a basis for a highly significant curriculum for teaching, as we saw earlier, but also a basis for true human community and communication. Our self-centeredness, however, gives us a natural pull away from attentiveness. But the Spirit of Christ Who, in drawing us to Him, draws us to one another, will make mutual attentiveness possible so that two-way communication will become a reality for us.

One current objection to this kind of mutual attentiveness travels under two guises: one is the possibility of being offensively nosy and intrusive; the other is the fear of really violating the privacy of other people. Certainly, privacy should be respected, and we should not force ourselves upon others, but attentiveness is not intrusiveness. Every human being wants to be known and to know as a person, and in ways that are both conscious and unconscious. We seek others that we may be known and may know. Attentiveness is really alertness to the lonely cry of man, and respects rather than violates the individual's separateness and sanctity.

Mutual Respect

Mutual respect is also a necessary quality in human relations. Respect for oneself and for others is not as common as one might expect. We find self-concern and some concern for others, but not respect. Respect for others is hard to maintain if one does not respect oneself, and it is appalling to realize what low estimates many people have of themselves. Although they may disguise from themselves and others their despair about themselves in many ingenious ways, lack of self-respect nevertheless is characteristic of many people's self-image. Their view of themselves results largely from their experiences in relationship, many of which we have already discussed. We may try to prevent the development of negative attitudes and feelings toward ourselves and our children, but no matter how loving we try to be, we shall inevitably cause some injury, distortion, and deprivation to the maturing person.

What, then, is the answer to this human problem? If the effect of growing up is to produce in us misgivings about ourselves and others, how can we acquire the self-respect and respect for others which is necessary for those who would truly serve God and man? Since mutual respect is a necessary condition for creative human relations, it is necessary that the vicious circle of non-respect be broken by someone. It is at this point that our participation in the re-creating life of God in Christ, which is made possible by the presence and work of His Spirit in us, makes a decisive difference in our self-estimate.

The Incarnation is the affirmation of God's faith in His creation. Christ is an expression of God's faith in man and what He is able to do through man. The principle of mutuality, which we have been affirming in our present discussion, is true not only for the relation between man and man, but between man and God as well. For the love of God in Christ affirms our value as persons in His desire to work through the people who will respond to His love, and shows His respect for what they can do. God's love and respect for men was expressed through the person of Jesus and continues to be expressed through persons in each generation. His people, the servants of His Spirit, are the ones who will break the vicious circle of mutual non-respect, and give the gift of mutual respect.

We can respect ourselves, therefore, because God shows His respect for us by loving and working through us. When we have a great task to do that calls for the courage and heroism of love, we can take a chance and set ourselves to the task because our faith in God makes it possible to have faith in ourselves and in those whom we would love. When we let our misgivings deter us so that we turn away from the challenges of love, we not only repudiate ourselves, but also turn our backs on God's affirming judgment of us.

Mutual respect has some identifiable characteristics. First, we must respect one another as autonomous, deciding persons. We cannot make our children and others do what we may think they ought to do. We can only meet them with whatever resources we have, and out of respect for their own power of decision and action leave them free to make their response. Then, when they have made it, we must respect it even though they may not be doing what we want them to do or doing it in the way we think best. Our decisions and way of life will not work for others.

We must also respect one another's dependence. But respect for others' dependence should not increase it; that is, we should try to meet their need, but not exploit it. Some years ago I was invited to lead a clergy conference on the subject of pastoral counseling. During the opening dinner before the beginning of the sessions, I sat next to a minister who tried to impress me with how much he knew about pastoral counseling. Among other things, he said, "You know, it's a wonderful thing to stand up before my congregation on Sunday morning and be able to count the increasing number of people who depend upon me for my pastoral care." The temptation to exploit human need is insidious, and we have all succumbed to it many times and in many ways. That pastor might better have rejoiced in those of his congregation who, in spite of their dependence and need, were able to use his help in their own independent way and thus grow stronger and more resourceful. Likewise, we may minister to the needs of our children and accept their dependence in ways that demonstrate our respect for them and our expectation that they will become more responsible.

Mutual respect also calls for respect of others who must answer for their own lives. While it is true that we are dependent upon God and His love for us, our response as individuals is a necessary complement to what He has done. The source of our life and of our redemption is in God, but we have to respond, and our responsible action makes complete what God has done for us. Therefore, we respect ourselves as having within ourselves the power of answer for our own lives. Mutual respect for one another as responsible beings increases our self-respect, and, conversely, our growing self-respect increases the respect we have for others.

Mutual Trust

Mutual trust is a third necessary quality in human life. As we saw earlier, nothing can happen in any relationship where there is not trust, and yet, lack of trust is everywhere prevalent. The great question is: How can we trust when we have such strong feelings of mistrust not only of persons, but also of the process of life? I have often had these misgivings as a teacher when, beginning with new students, I wondered how we could go through the crises of learning again. Where would I find the strength and courage for the challenges? Would they respond to their opportunities and resources? Parents have the same questions when they think of their children and wonder if, after all the years of care, they will turn out all right. Sometimes we become overwhelmed at the sheer weight and endlessness of our responsibilities, and in those moments we become profoundly discouraged. The need of love is desperate, and we feel wholly unequal to meeting that need. How wonderful it would be if we could have more confidence in ourselves and in others, and likewise in the processes of life to which we must commit ourselves. The answer to this longing is in the old, but ever new, affirmation that those who have faith in God can have faith in man and in the relationships of life.

As we read Paul's epistles to the Corinthians, we may notice that he seems to have been more confident of them than they were of themselves. Yet, his confidence in them was not so much in them as it was in the Holy Spirit. Because of the Spirit, he had reason to have confidence in what the Spirit would do among, in, and through them. Along this same line, a teacher made the following comment about his experience in one of his classes: "On one occasion I was suffering from some agenda anxieties, afraid that the members of the class, in the course of their discussion, would not arrive at some important and necessary insights. I was tempted to make sure that they saw certain things in the subject that I felt they ought to see, but fortunately I was restrained from interfering. Instead, I had an exciting morning hearing all the things that I wanted to say said by them. It was a great experience! This illustrates how important it is for us to keep ourselves from meddling, and to have confidence in the Spirit. Then the truth appears in the midst of us much more powerfully than if we handed it out, because when it appears out of the midst, it comes with authority, it comes with depth, it is memorable. The truth that comes to us in this way makes us free. The moral is obvious: Let us trust what God is trying to accomplish in us, and therefore trust one another."

To trust in the Spirit's working through dialogue does not mean that we shall be successful in all our endeavors. People's response to being trusted is not dependable or consistent. Man's response to God's trust, expressed in the life of Christ, produced the crucifixion. We all have had the experience of having our trust in others betrayed. This tempts us to become bitter, to lose faith in man, and to lose faith in God. But these responses are not a contradiction of trust; they are a part of the curriculum of trust. Trust, if it is to do its full work, must include mistrust, and faith must include doubt. I am helped to accept this insight because of the awareness of the doubt that is so much a part of my own faith which God accepts as a part of me and which gives my faith something to do. After all, faith is for doubt, courage is for anxiety, love is for hate. Instead of resenting hate, anxiety, doubt, and mistrust, we should accept them as a part of life.

We are called by the divine love to be lovers, called by God to be His servants, called by the Saving Person to be His person in the realm and the relationship of the personal. We are precious and important to one another and to God. We have a responsibility for others that must be met by our first being responsible for what we are in ourselves, the instrument for the revelation, in personal terms, of the power of love. It is imperative, therefore, that if we are to love others as we love God, we must love ourselves as being infinitely precious to God and ourselves, and indispensable because we have responded to a means of salvation for one another.

VI

LOVE IN ACTION

"By this we know love, that he laid down his life for us:
and we ought to lay down our lives for the brethren."—*1 John 3:16*

WE COME NOW to the climax of our study. Love must lay down its life; that is, it must give itself. The question then is: What is the mode and place of its self-giving? Under this heading I want to consider the nature of communication, evaluate the church as an agent of communication, and dwell on the implications of our study for church unity.

The Importance of Communication

Communication is essential to the expression of love and indeed to life itself. Where there is love, there must be communication, because love can never be passive and inactive. Love inevitably expresses itself and moves out toward others. When communication breaks down, love is blocked and its energy will turn to resentment and hostility. One of the greatest of tragedies occurs when the partners of a relationship break off their communication with each other. Without communication, the possibilities for a relationship become hopeless, the resources of the partners for the relationship are no longer available, the means for healing the hurts that previous communication may have caused are no longer present; and each, when he recovers from his need to justify himself and hurt the other, will find himself in a bottomless pit of loneliness from which he cannot be pulled except by the ropes of communication, which may or may not be capable of pulling him out again because of their weakened condition. Many of us know what it means to be in a foreign country where we cannot speak the language, but the loneliness of that condition is as nothing compared to the loneliness that is the product of an alienation that has been produced by either irresponsible use of the means of communication or a willful refusal to employ them.

If there is any one indispensable insight with which a young married couple should begin their life together, it is that they should try to keep open, at all cost, the lines of communication between them. Everyone needs and should have premarital counseling, if only to help them to this all important insight. Here is a place where the church's ministry needs to be strengthened, since so many people turn to the church to have their marriages solemnized. Before each marriage is performed, the minister should meet with the couple and help them prepare for the relationship, and he should include in that preparation the guidance that will help them to understand how indispensably important to its preservation, and, therefore, to their life together, are all the means of communication between them. Fortunately, more and more ministers are assuming this responsibility; and fortunately, also, more and more seminaries are providing instructions that teach ministers how to minister helpfully at this strategically important time. But much more needs to be done. Many marital breakdowns due to failure of communication could be alleviated, if not prevented, by giving young couples assistance when they are beginning their life together.

But communication is indispensable in all relationships, and not only in the personal ones like marriage. In labor disputes, for instance, the bargaining relationship breaks down when either one or both parties abandon the attempt to communicate with the other. Therefore, we may conclude, in paraphrase of the Scriptures: If any man says that he loves God and will not try to communicate with his brother, he is a liar!

But what is communication, and why is it so difficult to achieve? Most people seem to think of communication as getting a message across to another person. "You tell him what you want him to know." This concept produces a one-way verbal flow for which the term "monologue" is descriptive. Much of the church's so-called communication is monological, with preachers and teachers telling their hearers, both adults and children, the message they think they should know. The difficulty with monological activity is that it renders the hearer passive. It assumes that he is a receptacle into which the desired message may be poured. It eliminates the possibility of his active participation in the formulation of the message, and seems not to heed that a part of the message is in the person who is to receive it.

Those who have studied the dynamics of communication and the process by which it occurs are convinced that the monological principle is contradictory to the nature of communication, and as a method is the least effective. Reflective observation of our own learning indicates that communication is most effective when we become a part of the process and meet the message with our own content. Furthermore, the monological principle is not one that was used by our Lord. He, Who was the full incarnation of love, made people participants in the Good News that He proclaimed. We think, for example, of His conversation with the woman at the well, in the course of which she moved from her superficial understanding of water to His understanding of the water of life, wherein the meaning of her life was revealed to her. [1] Again, we think of the lawyer who put Him to a test by asking what he must do to inherit eternal life, and our Lord drew him out in such a way that he answered his own question. [2] The Gospels are full of such illustrations of our Lord's method of communication. It is curious, therefore, that the church has settled for the opposite monological principle which is quite unequal to the task of conveying the full meanings of the gospel.

Communication Is Dialogue

Our Lord's method, which we may call the dialogical, has been vindicated by modern research into the dynamics of communica-

[1] John 4:5 ff.
[2] Luke 10:25 ff.

tion, which has demonstrated conclusively that the to-and-fro process between teacher and pupil, between parent and child, provides the most dependable and permanent kind of education. What is that to-and-fro between one who knows and one who does not? The monological argument against the dialogical process is that the ignorant and untutored have nothing to contribute, so that the addition of zero and zero equals zero. This kind of comment, which is made by surprisingly intelligent and otherwise perceptive people, and all too often by educators, demonstrates how little they know about the processes of learning. Nor does it follow that the dialogical principle forbids the use of the monological method. There is a place for the lecture and for direct presentation of content, but to be most useful they should be in a dialogical context. Furthermore, it is quite possible for a person giving a lecture to give it in such a way that he draws his hearers into active response to his thought, and although they remain verbally silent, the effect is that of dialogue. As a matter of fact, one should not confuse the different methods of teaching with the dialogical concept of communication. Both the lecturer and the discussion leader can be either monological or dialogical, even though they are using different methods. The person who believes that communication, and therefore education, is dialogical in nature, will use every tool in the accomplishment of his purpose. When the question needs to be raised, he may use the discussion method or perhaps some visual aid. When an answer is indicated, he may give a lecture or use some other transmissive resource. But his orientation to his task is based on his belief that his accomplishments as a leader are dependent partly upon what his pupil brings to learning, and that for education to take place their relationship must be mutual.

What is it that the learner brings that is of such great value to the teacher? What possibly can the child have that the parent needs in order to help the child learn and mature? The child, and every person for that matter, brings to every encounter meanings drawn from his previous experience which, in one way or another, prepares him for what is to be learned. In Chapter IV we considered some of the early, basic acquisitions of the individual; for example, the meanings of trust and mistrust acquired in his first year, of liberating autonomy or resentful dependence, and other meanings which influence to a high degree his openness to the teacher and to what the teacher has to give. In addition to these basic meanings, he has a whole host of others which he has picked up from his previous experience: knowledge of people, of himself, of the world in which he lives, of the nature of things, all of which he uses in response to the approach of parent, teacher, friend, or whoever may be apt to confront him with new truth.

We need to remember that the meanings the learner brings are far from complete and mature, and that he is in the process of growing and becoming more adequate. He wants to learn, but he does not want to learn at the price of his own integrity. In learning he wants to have the sense of acquiring new powers. Any approach to him that seems to diminish him in any way closes him as a responsive, learning person. Furthermore, his experience thus far and its meaning produce in him questions for which he would like to have answers. The individual, therefore, brings to his meeting with others certain beliefs, attitudes, understandings, knowledge, and questions, which, in one way or another, have prepared him or closed him to learning. A good teacher, accordingly, pays attention to what his pupil brings.

The teacher (and here I am not thinking of the professional teacher only) first makes it his business to find out about his pupil or about the person with whom he wishes to communicate. As teacher, he needs to know as much about his pupil as he needs to know about his subject. He wants to help him ask his questions, so that what is communicated will be an answer to his questions. All too often what we offer as answers fail because they are addressed to questions which have not been asked, and, therefore, do not have meaning for them. The parent and teacher, therefore, should seek to call forth and formulate the understandings of children in order that they may more readily hear and understand the new truth that is being presented.

The need to be aware of the meanings that each person brings to his educational encounters is equally relevant to disagreements between adults. Many a husband and wife, for instance, fail to deal with a disagreement or quarrel constructively because each is thinking only in terms of the meanings he brings to the conflict, instead of trying also to discover the concerns and meanings his partner brings. We all know that sometimes the real cause of a quarrel is not expressed, with the result that the quarrelers can only deal with the superficial meanings of the conflict and in ways that further alienate them from each other. The responsibility for communication in such instances calls for each partner to pay attention to the meanings that the other one brings to the conflict, and try also to help the other say what he means, for his own and the sake of the other. In this way, constructive communication may be resumed.

The Purpose of Communication

The question now needs to be raised: What is the purpose of communication? There is a tendency on our part to regard consensus and assent as the goals of communication. The attempt to get people to sign on the dotted line, as it were, makes our communications aggressive and imperialistic. The hearer is not respected as an autonomous, deciding person, and this may cause him to decide against the message because of the alienating way in which it is being presented. When the gospel is preached without respect for the autonomy and integrity of the individual, the effect is alienating. The same results occur when parents act imperialistically in relation to the educational opportunities in the home.

The goal of communication is not to secure assent and agreement, but is, rather, to help the individual make a decision and translate it into action. We have to face the possibility that we may not like his decision, but that it may be the decision he must make now. For the moment, the child may say "No" to some admonition or instruction that his parent is giving him, which may seem like a breakdown and failure of communication. On the other hand, if it is the child's own decision and if the parent can respect it, while at the same time protecting the child from its unfortunate consequences, it may be a step in the process by which the child will eventually say "Yes." Reflection will reveal how often we have arrived at an affirmative response by the route of a negative one. The negative response was then seen as part of the process by which we moved toward accepting a truth.

Preparation for church membership of both young and old needs to employ this concept of communication. The instruction of many church members has been so ambiguous that they are not clear about what they have decided for or against. After all, we cannot say "Yes" to anything without also saying "No" to other things. People who are prepared for church membership should understand and be able to state the reason for the faith they affirm, and know what alternatives they rejected.

They need help also in discovering what their affirmations and denials mean for their way of life. Only then will they be able to make strong and enabling commitments. One reason for the uncertain witness of many so-called Christians and church members is that they have been persuaded to be Christians without either having that relationship or its alternatives explained to them. Young people in particular need help in knowing what they are choosing against in order that they may be unambiguously for what they have chosen. In an age when values are confused and people's need for clear-cut loyalties is great, it is tragic that the church's communication is confused. Let us try, therefore, to communicate in ways that will help people to speak their own "yeas" and "nays" with clarity and conviction.

The Agent of Communication

This thought brings us naturally to a consideration of the church as the agent of communication. The church, as the fellowship of the Holy Spirit, is the instrument that God created to speak and act for Him in each generation. Our human response to His calling us to be His people and servants produced the church as an institution, with its organizational and denominational divisions. As any perceptive person realizes, there is often conflict between the church as the fellowship of the Holy Spirit and the church as institution. As institution, the church faces the temptation of being more concerned about itself than about God and His purposes for His people. As we saw in Mr. Churchill's remarks, in Chapter I, the church can become so preoccupied with itself that it loses its sense of responsibility for its mission to the world. We saw also that the relationship between the church and the world is intended to be close, for the world is the sphere of God's action, and the church is the means of His action. The church, therefore, must be found at work in the world, and must feel within itself the tension between the saving purposes of God and the self-centered purposes of man. This is what might be called creative tension.

The maintaining of this creative tension requires that the church as institution be open constantly to the reforming vitality of the Holy Spirit, and church people should be open-minded, adaptable, and ready to live for God experimentally. They must be prepared to face the crises of life as they occur individually and socially with courage and a desire to lead the way for their fellow men. Instead of this, we find that church people have the reputation of being ultra-conservative, reactionary, and lovers of the status quo. The children of light, as it were, are being dragged along by the children of darkness, and are being compelled by them to face up to responsibilities which they ought to have assumed in the name of God years before anyone else. Of course, the record of the church is not altogether negative. In many places the leadership and the membership of the church have courageously pioneered the way in times of crisis and change. This experimental approach to life and crisis ought to be more characteristic of the church than it is. Where it does not exist, it is safe to assume that the membership is serving itself rather than the Spirit of God.

The church that is preoccupied with itself can no more express love for others than can a self-centered individual. Church members who are primarily concerned about the maintenance of a church and its educational unit on a particular corner in a certain town create a diseased organization. It suffers from a condition which, in an individual, would be called hypochondria. It is necessary, of course, for an individual to give some attention to his diet, cleanliness, and health in order that he may live his life and do his work. Likewise, the church needs to give some attention to its maintenance, for it needs to be nourished in its gathered life in order that it may do its work in its dispersed life.

The decisive role of the church is not in the church's church, but in the world: ministering to people at the beginning of and during their married lives, accompanying them in and through their marital failures, and helping them to learn from their experiences so that if they marry again they may do so with more understanding and resourcefulness; guiding them in the raising of their children, and helping them to correlate the insights of the social sciences that throw light on the nature and meaning of human development, especially the ultimate or religious meanings of that development; helping them find their place in the world's work with as much meaning as possible, and nurturing in them a faith and courage that makes it possible for them to face the conflicts, temptations, and sins of modern industrial life; standing by them in all the crises that they encounter in the course of their human existence; encouraging them to advance in company. with the most creative minds on the frontier of human exploration and experimentation; and fearlessly traveling with them as they wrestle with the changing value structures of each new generation, and guiding them in the use of their leisure. But most of all, in and through all of these ways, the church's task is to try to reveal to men that, though their identity in the world may be confused and lost, in their relationship with God they are known and loved. The church, as a fellowship of men, should exist not only to proclaim this truth in the abstract, but to live it in the sphere of the personal and social.

Various Concepts of Ministry

Every congregation and every member of a congregation needs to ask what image of the church governs its life, because our images can be idols that keep the church from being the instrument of God's action, and because that image can keep us from being persons in whom the Spirit of God can be incarnate. Such an examination calls for that sort of rethinking of our conception of the ministry that the Reverend Mr. Gates called for in our first chapter. The conception of the ministry held by both ministers and laymen will naturally reflect their conception or image of the church. Here both the ordained member and the lay member are caught in the grip of stereotypes that threaten to stifle the vitality of the church's ministry. Especially is this true in a time like our own, when the social order is undergoing radical changes.

All too often lay people assume that the problems of the ministry and of the church belong to the clergy alone. Many conscientious ministers today, erroneously assuming this responsibility, are confused as to what their role is. The problem of ministerial roles belongs to the whole church. It is not easy in this time of transition for ministers to be sure of what is expected of them. They sense or see clearly that the old images and patterns of the minister of the gospel do not fit the present time, and, therefore, are not safe ones to follow. Nor do the unsettled conditions of our civilization give very clear-cut clues for the formation of new and relevant concepts of the ministry. Consequently, many ministers, including far too many young ones, seek refuge in different stereotypes which fail to serve the church, and only provide them with the means of evading the real challenges of their task. What, then, are some of these stereotypes?

First, some ministers settle for a stereotype of the priesthood. They seek to recapture and transplant in our age an earlier and relevant priestly vitality that succeeds today only in assembling the dry bones or external forms of that role. Or, they may succumb to the preacher stereotype. Under the influence of that image, they think of the preacher as a performer, a sermon as a performance, and the congregation as an audience. That image is partly a product of the monological understanding of communication, and partly a result of the human need to justify oneself by an oversimplified function. The proclamation of the Holy Word as mere content and without dialogical intent is not true preaching of the gospel. Holy words were never meant to be used to justify ministerial function. The Word of God justifies us, but our words about the Word of God do not justify us. Furthermore, the Living Word did not enter the world imperialistically, and that Word should not be preached presumptively now, but with the expectation of having to engage the world responsibly. Still other ministers try to find a contemporary concept of ministry by modeling themselves after one of the respected patterns of our society: the business executive, the physician, or the group therapist. But as controlling images of the church's ministry, these are not comprehensive, and they too tend to become constricting stereotypes.

Then there is the stereotype of the local church, which is still thought of as a parish in a nineteenth-century neighborhood sense. In most places the parish community is no longer the center of people's common life. The neighborhood in which the church is located is an area to which people come home from their varied activities in order to sleep. And for an increasing number of men whose work keeps them on the road, even sleeping at home occurs only on occasional week ends. These and other stereotypes stifle the full power of the ministry and keep it from being equal to today's task. Too many ministers, in consequence, feel alone and separated from their people, and are bewildered by the complexity of their work and the ambiguous results of their efforts.

Lay people, on the other hand, receive little help in overcoming their stereotypes of the ministry and gravitate to a concept of the church that is hard to distinguish from a middle-class country club or a social service center. Another complicating influence is the current emphasis on the lay ministry. The general stress on the priesthood of all believers had made both clergy and laity less sure about the role of the clergy, even to the point, figuratively speaking, of seeming to unordain the ordained, and without clearly defining the ministry of the lay member.

Is there an answer to these confusions and ambiguities? What can clergy and laity now do to find their present and new role in the life of the church and world? There is an answer to these questions which, if followed, will open the ministry of the whole church to the renewing vitality of the Holy Spirit.

First, the role of the clergy and the concepts of it are the responsibility of the whole church. But the clergy are more conscious of the problems of the church and of the ministry, and they should, therefore, share them with the laity. Ministers make the mistake of keeping "their" problems, which are really the problems of the church, to themselves, instead of making sure that the rest of the church members are aware of and assuming responsibility for them.

Second, if the clergy are to share these concerns with the laity, they must break through the stereotypes held by both groups as described earlier. There is evidence that both ministers and laity are suffering restraints as a result of their false images of each other. The question is: Do the clergy dare to reveal themselves as spiritual leaders who do not always know the answers, and who themselves need desperately to be a part of a church that is a supportive and accepting fellowship? When asked why they do not discuss problems of the church within the church, ministers often reply: "What would my people think of me? I'm supposed to be the answer man." The truth is that many laymen welcome being released from false images of the clergy.

Third, ministers, therefore, need to be dialogists rather than monologists. This might turn out to be the appropriate concept of their role for this day. As representatives of the gospel, which was born of the full meeting and full interchange between God and man in Christ, the minister must learn to engage in dialogue with his people, and to participate in that dialogue with God which goes on in their living. The great questions of the church and the ministry are not going to be solved by the ordained ministers alone, but by the clergy and the laity accepting communication with each other as a part of their common ministry, and together bringing the gospel into dialogue with the world.

It is imperative that ministers and people talk to each other deeply, not about the housekeeping of the church, but about the church and its message, about its place in and relation to the world, and about its ministry, including the respective roles of clergy and laity. This kind of persistent, continuing talk is imperative for two reasons: first, it brings out and correlates the truth that is in man about these matters; and, second, the Holy Spirit reveals the truth of Christ to and through men who give themselves to each other in earnest search for the truth.

The Church and the World in Dialogue

We may conclude, therefore, that the problems of the ordained ministry in the world today are the problems of the church. Members of the church, including the clergy, must take the risks of communication, which are the risks of creativity, and talk with one another about their concerns. We must do this with the expectation that God will speak and act through our dialogue together, so that it will become our dialogue with Him. Out of this will come new insights and concepts for our respective roles, with a new awareness of our task for Christ in the world. It would seem, then, that our most effective starting point for a new and relevant image of ourselves for our task today is that of men who are in dialogue with God through their dialogue with their people. The spirit of this dialogue, however, must be the Spirit of Christ. The form of the ministry needs to be rethought in each age, but it must be formed by a double focus on Christ's ministry and the need of the world today.

Some of this dialogue, of course, has already been going on, and out of it certain insights have already appeared about the relation of the clergy and the laity. In the *gathered* church, with the focus on the worship, pastoral, educational, and organizational life, the ordained member is the chief minister and the lay members are his assistants. This does not mean that the lay people are working for the pastor and that their loyalty is to him. Instead, it means that both are working together for Christ and their loyalty is to Him. Within that relationship the congregation has called a member, usually trained and ordained, to direct it in performing the church's functions. The minister is entrusted, for example, with the educational work of the church. Some of his educational responsibility is delegated to the organization known as the church school. A few laymen are selected and professionally trained to be directors of Christian education; others from the congregation are trained to be the teachers, but, as such, they are serving as assistants to the one who is officially responsible for that activity. Likewise, when laymen are used in church visitation, they do so as assistants to the minister, to whom this official responsibility is delegated.

On the other hand, in the work of the *dispersed* church, which is active in and serving the world, the chief minister is the layman who, in the home or in the office, on the street or in the shop, in the school or in the university, or wherever the work of the world is going on, *is* the church in that situation and must be the minister of Christ there. The ordained man, in this aspect of the church's work, is the assistant or resource person.

This concept of the complementary relationship between the ordained and the unordained should inform the church's gathered life. The sermon, the preparation for church membership, all adult education programs, and the general ministry of the church, need to be conditioned by the thought that the purpose of the official teachers and preachers and administrators of the church's program is to prepare and guide the people of God in the performance of their work *in the world,* as representatives of Christ there. Resources need to be created in the church's program whereby people can come back from their ministry in the world, be helped to understand what has happened, and by reflection upon it learn how more effectively to be the church in the world. For this reason, seminars for parents need to be held in order that they may receive assistance in understanding their role as ministers of the church in the home. Seminars for businessmen and professional people also are indicated for the same reason. A point of focus for all church membership courses should be the question: When you become a member of the church, how are you going to exercise your ministry in the world? This orientation could be the source of a new evangelism that would make its witness heard in the depth and detail of human life.

The Reunion of the Church

We turn now to consider some of the implications of what we have been thinking for the reunion of the church. If the church is the instrument of God's action in the world, and its members are supposed to be the incarnations of His Spirit by means of which He accomplishes His purpose, the condition, as well as the concept of the church, is important. One of the tragedies of Christendom is the fact that the body of Christ is so divided and its parts live in such competitive relationship that the purposes of God are obscured and blocked. Movements toward reunion have borne fruit, with the result that some denominations have resolved their differences and reunited. But much more progress needs to be made, if the church is to be equal to the demands that modern life is making on it for spiritual leadership.

In each denomination there are clergymen and laymen who have erroneous concepts and understandings and expectations of the other denominations. I direct a training center which is attended by clergy and laymen from many denominations. These people often are surprised to discover, as a result of studying together the church's nature and purpose, how much they have in common. They discover that doctrinal differences are not as great as they had thought, that there are no denominational differences built into human nature or into human problems, and that they have many resources in common, namely, the God-given and redeemed resources of human relationships, the Scriptures, prayer, preaching, pastoral care, and teaching. Many of them have been heard to say, "I am glad to have had it revealed to me that in some ways our differences are more apparent than real." This kind of insight, however, is not possible unless a situation is created in which representatives of different denominations can begin to trust each other, and to think and communicate below the level of their differences. It is possible to do this, however, and more of it should be done. There is no reason why the local congregation should not invite neighboring congregations to come together with it for a study program for the purpose of finding their common brotherhood in Christ and their common responsibility for the community in which they live. A divided church does not make a good organ for the communication of love.

We come now to the distinctive contribution of our discussion thus far in this matter of the unity of the church. The work of reunion, of course, is the work of the Holy Spirit. But our response to Him in approaching reunion should be centered in a study of His purposes for the church *now* and *in the future,* rather than on a reconciliation of the *differences that occurred in the past.* It is exceedingly difficult to undo the mistakes of the past and to change the rigid images and patterns that have been forged by the misunderstandings of our predecessors. Merely trying to adjust them to each other will not do. It is something else again to be willing to change these by giving ourselves to a responsible consideration of what God wants His church to be and to do *now,* and thus attempt the reunion in response to present and future values.

The images that Presbyterians and Methodists and Episcopalians and Baptists and Lutherans now have of themselves might be changed, thus making possible changes in their images of one another, and this would certainly open the way to deeper levels of communication. Instead of this, we have members of different denominations thinking rather rigidly about themselves and others. Our identities and responsibilities are accepted in terms of differences that were laid down in the past, and may be held independently of what God may be wanting His church to do in this moment. The church is not the Kingdom of God; it is not the end of God's action. It is a means to an end, and, as circumstances of human life change, it is not inconceivable that God would like to have us make changes in that instrument for man's salvation which He created.

Proposals for the reunion of the churches often arouse the fear that our respective denominations, to which we are devoted, will be replaced by what some conceive of as a "superchurch." Such an arbitrary replacement of church organization is not the objective of the unity movement. Instead, we should respond to the Spirit's prompting to keep our denominational loyalties subject to our loyalty to Him, in order that we may be open to whatever form of church life and action the Spirit may indicate for our generation. We are concerned about the church as the body of Christ in our time. As His body, we must find our unity in Him; but this may mean that we shall have to abandon some things that have seemed good. Some words of our Lord are hard to bear: "He who loves father or mother more than me is not worthy of me." [1] These words of our Lord are equally applicable to all other relationships, including our denominational ones. It does not follow, however, that our denominational devotion is of itself disloyal to Christ, any more than our devotion to our loved ones is disloyal. We do need, however, to make sure that we love and serve Him, and not something or someone else. Our concepts of ourselves and of others may need to be changed.

The changing of these images of ourselves and of others is not a responsibility that belongs only to our top-level church leaders. Every Christian in every church in every part of the world must

[1] Matt. 10:37.

share it, because each person has a specific responsibility for his relationship with his Christian brothers, by whatever name they may call themselves. The parent who seeks to exercise his ministry in his relationship with his child needs also to be open to his responsibility as a member of some historic branch of the Christian church for the welfare of that church and the relationship of its separate parts. We cannot accept what we have inherited in the form in which we inherited it. Our inheritance in many ways is precious and wonderful, but our human response can deform it. Our church can be a means of fulfilling our discipleship, but it can also be an obstacle to it. Therefore, our membership and participation in a denomination needs to be kept under the constant judgment of God in order that we as members may serve Him more loyally.

We are Christ's, brought into this relationship by His love, and we can grow in this relationship only as we are guided by His Spirit. Everything else is secondary to this. But all other relationships, if offered to Him and illumined and corrected by His Spirit, can be wonderful also, because then they too become a part of His means of reuniting, by His love, men with one another and with Him.

"In this is love, not that we loved God but that he loved us and sent his Son. . . . We love, because he first loved us." [1]

[1] 1 John 4:10, 19.